Francis Nenik
Sebastian Stumpf
SEVEN PALMS

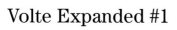

Volte Expanded #1

TEXT
FRANCIS NENIK

PHOTOGRAPHY
SEBASTIAN STUMPF

SEVEN PALMS

THE THOMAS MANN HOUSE IN PACIFIC PALISADES, LOS ANGELES

SPECTOR BOOKS

Francis Nenik
SKIPPING ALONG THE BLANK SPACES

1550 San Remo Drive—A Room Tour
or
If You Want Action, Start on Page 45

There is no one at home. The flow of their habits and an irresistible desire for meat have driven the residents of the villa outdoors, and the Californian climate has done the rest … Thomas Mann is in Westwood for a haircut, his wife Katia tries to get the leanest cut of beef at the market, and the maid has the day off and is lying on the beach in Santa Monica. Who would blame her? Her room is on the ground floor, directly under the balcony, in permanent shade. And then there's the garage, which borders directly on her tiny empire and has a wall so thin you not only hear the cars but can almost smell their exhaust. The air in the maid's room is stifling and stagnant—perhaps that's why she's left the window open. But it's not her fault. She couldn't have known that I was going to drop by and climb in.

The Maid's Room
A linoleum floor. This is the very first thing you notice when you stand on the windowsill and try to jump over the bathtub. Getting into the tub isn't an option because it's still wet and I don't want to leave any traces. Nor do I want to have to remove any. I just want to wander through the rooms for a bit before their occupants return to fill them with life again. Besides, being a good burglar-detective, I brought the building plans and have informed myself not only about the property but also about the individual rooms and the peculiarities of the interior, and therefore I know that all the private rooms of the villa have oak floors, except for the maid's room. The owner decided that linoleum would be good enough here. He also paid close attention to subtle differences in other areas and had the architect mark them clearly in the building plan.
"ALL CLOTH-POLES IN CLOSETS AND WARDROBES EXCEPT MAID'S ROOM TO BE CHROME PLATED‼," it says, and on the next

page the instructions continue: "ALL DOORS IN MAID'S ROOM, BATH #4 & GARDEN FURN. STORAGE TO BE 1-PANEL DOORS. FRAME TO HAVE NO MOULDING!!!"

The room itself barely measures thirteen by thirteen feet, and if it weren't for the adjoining washroom and the small closet next to it, the maid would find it difficult to store her belongings. The room is definitely too small for two people, especially since its furniture—a bed, two wardrobes, a table, chairs, and the dressing table in the corner—already takes up a large part of the space. Books, on the other hand, are absent, and shelves are also missing. But clothes and shoes are scattered all over the floor, and even the radio on the small bedside table seems to have been placed there somewhat casually. It rests on a pile of magazines, its handle flipped up. It looks as if the maid has only just acquired the radio.

Apart from that, there's not much to see. The room serves the girl as the girl serves the house. That her room should be in the shade is all a part of it and cannot be changed. At least the stuffy air can escape through the open bathroom window. The only thing she can't get rid of is the room's strange chill. Maybe that's why there's a wall heater next to the door. It looks like a big old intercom made of iron, with a fire burning inside. There's one in the bathroom, too. It's mounted opposite the washbasin and warms the maid's backside during her morning wash.

The Kitchen

It is said that the architect of the house was actually an interior designer, and that he learned his trade outfitting ocean liners. He was, therefore, someone who understood how to make perfect use of space and wouldn't shy away from asking customers about their dress sizes in order to be able to precisely measure cabinet drawers and wardrobes.

II

To be honest, I thought the whole thing about perfectly made-to-measure furniture was a modern myth, the kind of joke that people tell each other in lofty rooms at architects' parties. But now that I'm actually inside Thomas Mann's kitchen, I can see that the architect measured everything in the house on San Remo Drive very carefully indeed and really went wild on the washbasin's cabinet, even though this time it was toe length rather than folded garments that he obsessed about.

But let's go one step at a time, starting at the south end of the kitchen and circling the room counterclockwise. That will give me a bit more time to roam at my leisure before the freshly coiffed master returns.

On the south side of the room is a cupboard for pots and pans, two feet wide by six and a half feet high. To the left of cupboard is the refrigerator, which everyone here refers to only as the "Frigidaire"—a massive white slab, which is much deeper than the surrounding cabinets and protrudes far enough into the room that the cupboards hanging on the wall to its left, and the base cabinets behind it, can hardly be seen.

I don't know why, but it seems almost as if the architect were secretly arranging a therapeutic family constellation here. On the far right is the long, tall cupboard of Thomas Mann; the refrigerator next to it symbolizes his wife; and the six cabinets to the left are their children, some of them hanging above and others below, all of them easily named—Erika, Klaus, and Elisabeth are the upper ones, Golo, Monika, and Michael the lower.

At any rate, on the east side of the kitchen is the gas stove. It's not just any stove, but a Thermador Range made of stainless steel with extra-wide hobs, two ovens of different sizes, and thick burners—a classic of American design and so stylish that *California Arts & Architecture* magazine dedicated an article to it in 1940. But that's not all, because the kitchen fitters have installed Andrew Orear's patented hood above the stove, a product of the Trade-Wind Motorfans Corporation, fully chromed and connected to the Californian sky via a sturdy duct — a technical marvel of which there is literary evidence, in keeping with the house itself, even if in this case it didn't feature in a light and airy art magazine, but on the sober pages of *Western Machinery and Steel World*.

Not to worry. If the hood shouldn't work for some reason or other, there are still quadruple casement windows on the north side of the kitchen, eleven feet six inches wide by four feet three inches high, large enough to exchange the smell of cooking for that of California.

As befits a kitchen, under the window there are three rows of tiles with two sinks underneath, fitted into a matching metal base unit. Not the most obvious place for an architect to make his mark, but this one is more concerned with precision than pomp. At the point where the base of the sink touches the floor, the building plan stipulates "2½ inch Toespace."

Thankfully, it isn't my job to analyze the Mann family's toe lengths. I am here to reflect on the house and its furnishings. To understand the story behind it, it is better to concentrate on the drawers and cupboards to the left and right of the sink, which provide storage space for all kinds of kitchen utensils, as well as room for cleaning supplies like buckets, dustpans, and brooms. But there's more: right next to the sink unit, there's a small door embedded in the wood, hiding a towel rack with four chrome bars. According to the building plan, this is a product of a company called "K-V"—which must be the initials of Knape & Vogt, and leads me to that household-goods manufacturer from Grand Rapids, Michigan, the self-proclaimed "furniture capital" of America, which has succeeded in placing its towelrack model number 798 at 1550 San Remo Drive.

On the other, far-left side of the sink, there is another door from which, when opened, a fully galvanized garbage can swings out, its swivel arm designed in such a way that, according to the building plan, it is "ant-proof," just like the unit housing the "revolving cooler," which is located to the right of the sink next to the window and contains the family's fruits and vegetables. Supposedly this entire cabinet is secured against the small creepy-crawlies from top to bottom. But I don't believe it. I imagine that things take a different course, that the ants blaze a trail and take over the house of the great writer. It will be a silent, slow, imperceptible takeover. But then, one day, when Thomas Mann has long since passed away and his former home is a mere piece of real estate for speculation, the newspaper will tell you all about this takeover. It will say, "The timber has been attacked by ants, meaning the wall and floor panels will have to be replaced." And at that moment some people who care about culture will try to undo the ants' takeover, in order to preserve something that has long ceased to exist.

The Laundry Room
I'm standing in the laundry room, and there's a problem. Thomas Mann doesn't mention this room anywhere, nor does anyone else. But that's not my problem. My problem is the washing machines, because there are none. The building plan contains two of them, but something happened between the architect making the specifications and the family moving in: the Japanese attacked Pearl Harbor and America stopped producing washing machines. Why not?! After all, war is not a clean affair, and those with servants can have their dirty laundry washed by hand. War as an opportunity to revive the good-old days. When the maid returns from the beach, she will recognize the lines of the waves in the ribs of the washboard.

The Storeroom between the Laundry Room and Kitchen
There is no way to get from the laundry room to the storeroom; you can only enter the storeroom from the outside. The shortest route

would be to climb through the laundry-room window and walk through the door on the left. It isn't locked, and the little conifer standing next to the door only pretends to be guarding the room behind it.

Inside the storeroom, there is nothing but garden furniture and gardening equipment. It is completely full, and that there should be any room at all is due to the fact that the table-tennis table, which is usually also stored here, is currently on the veranda.

Thomas Mann calls it the "ping-pong" table. When the children first set it up on the veranda after moving in, he was so pleased with the sight that he noted it in his diary. He never actually plays himself, nor is he interested in any other sport. The sentence "Pretty view from the living room onto the veranda where the young people play ping-pong" is his most detailed sports reportage.

He makes no mention of the storeroom, and I'm not even sure if he's ever set foot inside it. Nevertheless, there is a storeroom that does play a role, if not for him, then for someone he knows, someone he tried to extract from just such a closet.

That closet, however, wasn't here in the villa, but in a run-down boarding house in Nice, France. There, in a small garden house, which really was little more than a storeroom for old furniture and all kinds of rubbish, the writer Alfred Wolfenstein lived and waited to be granted permission to leave for America. Thomas Mann vouched for him, submitting a letter of recommendation in March 1942 and insisting that Wolfenstein's application for immigration be dealt with "benevolently and with the appropriate urgency." Wolfenstein even had the correct permits to leave the country. But things didn't work out. It was too late. Large parts of France were occupied by the Germans and the rest was under the control of the Vichy regime, and so

Wolfenstein, a Jew, could do nothing but hide in the storeroom in Nice and make it his home—a home where he lived, worked, and wrote while the powers that be played ping-pong with the world. But Alfred Wolfenstein gradually became ill, and when he took his own life on January 22, 1945, Thomas Mann didn't hear anything of it. How would he have? Wolfenstein was only a small ping-pong ball in the game of the great powers, one that missed the table, rolled into a corner, and at some point stopped moving.

It's a strange feeling. There is an architect who pays attention to every last detail in the construction of the house, who measures and plans everything—and then there's the world, Europe, the war, which he couldn't factor in even if he wanted to. But in the end, the difference isn't all that big; it fits into this storeroom, between the tools and furniture. Because, as confined as it may be in here when you turn around and look through the doorway, you can still see the sea. "Sea View" was also the name of the guesthouse in Nice where Alfred Wolfenstein lived for several months in the garden shed between rakes and spades, waiting in vain for a chance to leave the country.

The Pantry

One would assume that someone who wrote tens of thousands of pages in his life and could describe everything and everyone with great clarity would have said something about his pantry. Strangely, this isn't the case. However, Thomas Mann did mention his family's previous storerooms and knew their significance. For instance, in 1918, when he feared that looters might ransack the family home and drag bags of food from the Munich villa, he wrote in his diary: "Katia and the children clear out the pantry and hide three-quarters of the supplies in different parts of the house." Other pantries pop up throughout Mann's writings, and even his wife Katia wrote about what was going on in them.

Only Mann's pantry here on San Remo Drive has gone without mention, and it looks as if the home's architect didn't have many ideas about it either. On the west side of the room, there is nothing but some standard cupboards: three big doors at the bottom and three small ones at the top, behind them supplies and inventory in common quantities and sizes.

On the opposite wall, finally, four wall-mounted cabinets: common commercial models, including a matching sideboard. The sideboard has a maple work surface with a small sink in its middle featuring a simple plastic splash guard at its rear. The sideboard comprises a series of drawers. The lower ones contain tablecloths, napkins, candles, and other household items; the upper ones are reserved for the family silver. The architect had apparently informed himself about the quantity and significance of the latter and made sure that there would be ample space inside the sideboard—he signaled this in the building plan with explanatory words and arrows. Hidden between standardizations, this note was a little sign to indicate his recognition that he wasn't building this house for ordinary people, but for "that amazing family."

The Dining Room

From the pantry, there is a door to the dining room. Compared to the wide sliding slab door on the other side, which leads into the living room, this door appears downright tiny, and when you enter the dining room from this side, you almost feel a little lost, because as soon as you open the door, you notice that it is situated in a corner of the room, and it almost seems as if someone tried to hide the door there. But it is in this location for a reason, because it marks the transition from the utility wing to the residential part of the house.

This is the oak-floor territory. Unfortunately, the family has had carpets fitted over the lumber, so the flooring is no longer visible, but it can still be clearly felt as you walk across it, and if you stand in one spot and rock a little you can even hear the familiar sound of creaking floorboards.

But who knows? Maybe it's supposed to be this way, maybe the architect had the flooring installed like this so that it would make precisely this noise to imbue the house with a sense of history—a hidden and yet clearly audible reminder of the Europe the family came from and the venerable houses they used to reside in.

The white-painted walls, on the other hand, are decorated with brocade carpets as well as Chinese-style fabrics and embroidery. Additionally, there is a large cupboard with Royal Copenhagen porcelain and a sideboard flanked by two floor-standing candelabra with seven white candles on either side. More candelabra are found on the sideboard itself, along with vases and silverware.

The center of the room, however, is marked by a long rectangular table that resembles a banquet table and can accommodate up to twelve people. But the seating chart is clearly regulated: whoever is closest to the master sits next to him at the table.

But now there is nobody here, and the table is bare except for an empty glass that apparently contained orange juice, as there are still remains of pulp around the rim. Meanwhile, the bock beer for lunchtime is waiting on the sideboard, along with coffee mugs and a bottle of liqueur.

This room's most important feature is the gong. Katia Mann strikes it when the cook has finished preparing lunch and the maid is ready to serve it. Then they flock from all corners of the house, sit down at the table and reach for the cutlery, eager to discover what may be on offer today.

But there is also another gong, even if nobody in the house knows anything about it. And yet it is there and it will beckon two persons to the Mann family — it will direct them from wooden barracks in the Sierra Nevada to this house on San Remo Drive.

The Living Room

A huge room, almost 550 square feet in size. Unfortunately, I have to share it, because I am not the only one who's here without permission. A huge lizard has made itself comfortable in front of the fireplace. From the looks of things, it's not the first time it's been here and it seems accustomed to the presence of humans — it doesn't pay attention to me, at least, and is instead absorbed in contemplating the painting hanging over the fireplace. It's Thomas Mann's favorite painting, *The Well* by Ludwig von Hofmann, and as we know Californian lizards like to stay in warm places near water.

Not far from the fireplace there is a sofa upholstered with floral motifs, and judging by the tracks, the lizard has made itself comfortable there before, too. It's ignored the rest of the furnishings (a flat coffee table, a few armchairs, a piano, a floor lamp), and the paintings by old German masters on the wall don't seem to be of any further interest to the reptile, nor does the large, heavy Empire cabinet, which houses the entire *Encyclopædia Britannica* behind its glass doors.

To the left of the fireplace, there is a combination radio-turntable system the size of a veritable kitchen counter. The radio is at the top, the record player is in a compartment below it, and the records are stored underneath that. But the lizard doesn't care for music. It's only interested in the painting — and also, a little bit, in me. It just gave me a look, at least, that didn't make me think it was particularly happy about my presence. But I wasn't planning on staying much longer, anyway. The only question is, In which direction should I continue my tour of the house?

The two large glass doors leading to the south and east terraces are tempting, but I don't want to be seen outside. Besides, the lizard's tail points to the small door that lies between the two, and maybe this is meant as a friendly hint to not just disappear, but to leave the room in this direction if I would, quietly, because the animal would like to sink its eyes back into contemplating *The Well*. At least from behind the door I shouldn't bother it anymore, since the architect has specified a "solid door" in his drawing and instructed the carpenters to use wood at least two inches thick. It seems that when planning the house, he even took into consideration the whims of art-loving lizards.

The Passage
From the living room, it's just a short walk to Thomas Mann's study. On the left, there is a large shelf full of books, and on the right two pictures hang on the wall. There is no way of telling what they show, for the window in the passage is covered with thick curtains. There is no place for the Californian sun here—and rightly so, since it shines on the present only. The passage, however, is a time tunnel. A space shuttle. A way back to Europe. An entrance to the world of literature. A portal to Thomas Mann's innermost thoughts. It is opened by a simple door.

The Study
Where do you start in this room? There is a large desk, an armchair, a sofa, two floor lamps, a grandfather clock, a side table, and a few framed pictures on the wall. In front of the windows, there are venetian blinds; behind the windows, there are palm leaves. Otherwise, the room is full of books from top to bottom. Basically, it's an ordinary upper-middle-class study in a well-appointed neighborhood, even if you can't just wander in here since that would mean breaking into the house a second time: "If Thomas Mann wants to deal with people, he comes out himself." Right now, however, Thomas Mann is dealing with his hairdresser (or maybe it's the other way around)

and has therefore not only left his study, but also the house, which was another reason I decided to enter it.

It's a wonderful sensation to amble through this room. The fitted carpeting and the runners atop it swallow every sound, and the oak planks underneath are as thick as they are solidly placed. With the walls, however, corners have been cut. In contrast to the house's other walls, they are not plastered on the inside but only paneled with wood — more or less, since they are basically nothing but plywood panels with a layer of fine-looking veneer, a solution usually chosen by an architect whenever a client's budget can't keep up with his symbolic ambitions.

The oak bookcases in front of the plywood walls are fortunately much more solid and all shelves can also be adjusted in height, although the architect made sure that the standard was maintained here as well. The brackets and bars under the shelves were all made by Knape & Vogt, whose products apparently not only hold towels, but also a German scholar's entire library.

But even in an extensive library, what really matters is orderliness. In other words, the task was to take into account the writer's visual desire for harmony, which is why all the shelves have been positioned so that the bookcase on the northern wall looks exactly like the one on the west wall. Such harmony goes even further, however, down to the smallest detail … "All grain vertically," say the building plans, and this instruction has indeed been followed.

There are additional bookcases under the large windows on the south and east sides, but unlike the others, they have sliding doors. Their shelves provide storage space for all sorts of things, although the architect has also made suggestions here and even indicated "space for … firewood" in one place. But there is nothing but paper piled up there now, because the proposed fireplace fell victim to budget constraints during the house's construction. Nevertheless, light is amply provided, as a more than thirty-foot-long lightwell has been fitted directly above the two shelving units on the room's north and west sides, containing almost two dozen concealed fluorescent lamps.

In fact, the architect has given free rein to his penchant for all kinds of different light fixtures, integrating everything that was technically feasible into the villa: indirect light, spotlights, spotlights recessed in the floor, classic chandeliers, floor lamps—you will find all of this in the house. Two different ceiling heights have been used on the first floor to ensure that it really comes into its own and that each room is able to provide the intended lighting in the best possible way.

In the study, however, the light, like the intellect, was elevated and placed above the bookshelves in the form of a conduit—the perfect design to provide enlightenment while writing, even when the venetian blinds shut out the Californian sun …

The Heater Closet

I leave the study, turn right and left, and am standing in the heater closet—or, to be more precise, in front of a heating system that warms the air in the house by means of a burner, adds a breeze of fresh air from outside, and distributes this mixture over the entire house by a series of ducts. On the whole, this is a clever machine, but unfortunately it's a bit susceptible to breakdowns, which is why the heating tends to blow cold air into the rooms, especially on cool days—and sometimes even sends a little burnt smell behind it.

"Check furnace size P. C.," the architect noted in the building plan, but it seems the heating engineers were fed up with his incessant instructions and fitted whatever they had at hand.

The architect, however, seems to have anticipated this. At least he's taken precautions and made sure that they can't access all the rooms, by building a secluded space behind the boiler room—one that no-body can enter, not even me, because there are no doors, windows, or other openings. It is an enclosure known as a "plenum space," an air-filled room designed exclusively to support the heating system.

It has the shape of a right-angled triangle with its tip pointing east—toward Europe.

But I have no intention of going to Europe. I want to explore this house. And so I exit the boiler room, ignoring both the small store-room to its left (there's nothing but junk in it, anyway) and the wash-room set in a corner to its right. Then I come across a staircase. It is quite steep and seems to have been designed especially for this nar-row space—and yet it is a copy. The architect has built one like this before, in the Stothart House, a two-story villa just a mile from San Remo Drive on the other side of the Riviera Country Club. But no-body here knows about this. The architect hasn't told anyone about the stairs, and I don't care. Maple steps and a metal banister lead me up to the second floor.

Thomas Mann's Bedroom

A strangely barren room. A bed, a bedside cabinet, a rocking chair, a mirror, an armchair, and a side table with nothing on it. At first glance, there are no books to be seen, only a few adventure novels that are hidden from prying eyes in a small niche behind the staircase. To the right of the staircase, there is a wide door leading out onto the terrace. But there's nothing to see there. The terrace is empty. Three hundred and forty-four square feet of free space—and the most interesting thing is the storm drain.

It is made of cast iron, expertly secured to the ground, and has a re-
movable sieve with a patented tension ring and capacious sediment
bowl. According to the building plan, it is a product of the Josam
Manufacturing Company of Michigan City, a small town in the state
of Indiana. The drain's model number is 454G. Its task is to catch
rainwater that collects on the terrace and to channel it back into the
ground using the gutter on the exterior wall of the study below, but
as long as the sun is shining, its work is suspended.

Back in the house, I am struck by the feeling that the bedroom is an
indoor extension of the terrace. A feeling of emptiness permeates the
room, which in spite of its furnishings seems somehow bleak and
impersonal, even if (or maybe because?) the wallpaper and curtains
have been chosen by the author himself, and the bed is covered with
the silk blanket that accompanied Thomas Mann for many years and
conceals the unfulfilled part of his nights.

Next to the bed, on the floor, a radio. A small appliance, similar to
the one in the living room. The frequency control is set to 1,070 kHz:
KNX Radio, home of the *Jack Benny Show*, which Thomas Mann
loves to listen to and which he receives crystal clear, even on foggy
days. The KNX broadcasting tower is located just a few miles from
here, down on Sunset Boulevard, transmitting its waves up into the
hills with a lush 50,000 watts.

Above the radio, on the wall, a painting. It's a print, a copy of Van
Gogh's *Portrait of a Young Farmer*, since once upon a time real farmers toiled here, on what is now Thomas Mann's property. Their task
was to cultivate the land for the coming sale of these lots. So they
came and ploughed the entire property just before construction com-
menced, forcing the architect to add a large "NOTE" to his drawings
and to point out to the builders that the elevation in his plan was no
longer correct and that the virgin soil only began about a foot down.

He couldn't have guessed that in Thomas Mann's bedroom it would be exactly the other way around, and that the room would be dominated by something impalpable, a tidy austerity, like a silk blanket that someone's spread over a freshly made bed and smoothed out before leaving again.

Thomas Mann's Bathroom

Behind the bedroom is Thomas Mann's bathroom, which contains the toilet, a washbasin, and a bathtub, six feet long and fully enameled—a real blessing, and not to be compared with the rubber trough that Hermann Hesse lent him a few years ago while Mann was exiled in Switzerland.

Thomas Mann's Dressing Room

A small room. Cabinets left and right. And above, on the ceiling, a hatch. It takes you out into California. But I don't want to go there now.

Katia Mann's Bedroom

An almost square room, much bigger than Thomas Mann's and also considerably fuller. A large bed, a chest of drawers, a small desk, a bookshelf—and letters everywhere. Only the cot by the wall is untouched by them. A small island in a sea of paper. With maple bars.

The letters are all addressed to Thomas Mann, but his wife is the one reading them. She also replies when matters fall into her domain. For this purpose, she's purchased a typewriter and placed it on the table between the stacks of paper. Basically, there is only one place on the desk that isn't covered in paper, and it looks as if there was a radio in that spot until very recently. At least the corresponding radio guide lies open next to it, and a program is marked with a cross.

Katia Mann's Bathroom

An expansive room, three times the size of Thomas Mann's bathroom. On the right, in a recess about six feet wide, there is a shower cubicle, diagonally opposite a large bathtub with a tiled shelf, a washbasin, various cabinets and mirrors, and, at the very back, in the corner, the toilet.

Outside the window, flowers grow in a box. You can pick them from the toilet—just sit there, do what has to be done, and make a floral garland. Or stick the flowers into your hair one by one. This is California, after all. Or at least it could be.

Katia Mann's Dressing Room

When I want to enter, it strikes me that the dressing table itself is not situated in the dressing room. The room is simply not big enough, so the chest of drawers has found its place outside to the right, still in the bathroom. In the dressing room itself, there are wardrobes on the left and right and opposite the door. We meet two old acquaintances—Knape & Vogt—this time in the form of a shoe rack. Model number 784 is firmly screwed to the wall, as required in the building plan, and consists of three rows of metal rods, slightly curved outward and coated with a nickel-chromium alloy, which together can accommodate up to twelve pairs of shoes. And the best thing is the patented "toe guards," which protect the toes even when they are not in the shoes. It seems that the architect has really thought of everything.

A First Guest Room

I leave the room and walk out into the hallway. There is a staircase in front of me, but a pungent smell draws me to the left.

A narrow corridor opens to a bright room behind it. The wall heater on the right is the same as in the maid's room. However, up here there is plenty of sun. And fresh air: the southern side of the room consists only of windows, a thirteen-foot-wide veil with a door leading to the balcony. And on the balcony, flowers. Multiple planters full of them, along the entire south-facing side — even in front of the large pane of satin glass that closes the balcony to Katia Mann's bedroom and cannot be seen through because of its frosted appearance, before which someone has placed a planter full of geraniums.

The top of the balcony is covered by a wooden pergola spanning its entire length. It gives the balcony the appearance of a veranda. However, the pergola only runs to half the width of the balcony, because the architect didn't want to leave the wall exposed. He can't stand it when water runs down the walls. So he had the roof protrude a good meter over the house. An exposed overhang doesn't look good on a pitched roof, however, so the underside was horizontally leveled and covered with wooden panels, creating a long rectangular surface called a "soffit." On one side it's anchored in the house wall; on the other side, it's connected to the upper end of the pergola. And yet there is a difference, because while the wood of the pergola is painted white, the soffit is plastered and finished in blue, as though it were an imitation of the Californian sky — an everlasting summer over the balcony. The room itself, on the other hand, has a somewhat cool appearance. A bed, some chairs, a simple table, the usual books. Various shelves and wardrobes are overflowing with shoes, papers, and clothes. But there is one more thing, something that's been there all along. It's a sweetish scent. It seems to have permeated the entire room, and can even be smelled outside on the balcony. Apparently, it's paraldehyde. This must be Erika Mann's room.

Thomas Mann's eldest daughter is addicted to the stuff. It's a sleeping pill that also works as a sedative. Ten milliliters is enough, and you dive into a deep twilight, no matter how much the Californian sun may blaze outside. But there's a problem. If you take the stuff for years, your bones grow soft.

On the other hand, in the Mann family there is a pronounced sense of irony, and who knows, a few softened bones may be just the price paid willingly by those who treat themselves and others with a certain harshness.

Another Bathroom …
… Therein a tub with a shower, a toilet, a washbasin, a mirror cabinet holding all the usual items. And onward …

A Second Guest Room
Things begin to repeat themselves, from the big to the small and back again. The "wall heater" in the wall to the right, the wide windows to the south, the shoe rack number 784 in the dressing room. And yet something is missing from this room. In contrast to the other rooms, there are no fictional works to be found here, only historical and political ones. The books themselves are all neatly lined up on the shelves, none of them are lying sideways, and nothing spills from the wardrobes. Every item has its place, everything contributes to the order of things, and there is only one newspaper that attracts my attention. It is lying on the table at the front left of the window, and a headline can be glimpsed on its sunlit front page. It is written in large bold letters and spreads across the entire page as if its appearance alone were intended to disturb this room's order. The content of the headline does the rest, as it manages to confuse the eager reader with just a few words: "President Truman is found drunk in St. Patrick's Cathedral, demanding that Eleanor Roosevelt dance naked for him."

A Third Guest Room
The last upstairs room. It looks abandoned. It doesn't look as if anyone lives here. Rather, it has the appearance of a room that is offered to guests for overnight stays on weekends. A sleeping place for the restless who are planning to move on soon.

When you open the door, you face a wall. It closes off the house to the west. Originally, there was to be a superstructure above the garage behind this wall, but that idea was abandoned. "Story over garage removed," the builder wrote in the "Application to Alter, Repair, Move or Demolish," and that's what happened. This might be why they didn't put a window in this wall: they thought that there would be a room behind it.

Now there is nothing there, neither a room nor a window, and there is nothing on the south side either. Only from the north does a little light enter the room, and a breath of fresh air flows in as well because the window is slightly open. This is lucky for me because otherwise I wouldn't hear that a car is pulling up the driveway. They're coming. They're coming back …

... so off you go, down the hall.
                              stair
                                 case
                                    down,
                                        out the back door

there is no one at home ...

Places don't tell stories. And if they do, the stories they tell aren't the ones you expect. The history of a place doesn't lie in what you may find there, but rather in what you find when you stay away.

I never visited the Thomas Mann House in Pacific Palisades.
I have no intention of ever going there.
I just feel like telling the story of this house.
I will scour libraries and archives for the ordinary and the absurd.
I'm going to spin yarns out of the rays of California's magnificent sun.
I'll skip along the blank spaces.

Nameless People Drift In and Out of Sight, and a Poet Is Finished Off

On July 21, 1941, Thomas Mann meets Friedrich Schiller. It's the most American yet of his evenings in Californian exile. When he enters Friedrich Schiller's property, he finds that the landlord has made a bonfire in the yard and installed a barbecue over it — a large, round grate hanging by a chain from a tripod, with pieces of boneless meat lying on it. Schiller says he has prepared a chicken dinner for his guest.

Thomas Mann is somewhat taken aback by the barbecue swinging back and forth in the evening breeze, as well as by Friedrich Schiller's casual greeting, but after expressing his gratitude for the invitation he sits down on one of the two chairs that are sitting in the garden as if by accident. As he looks around, he discovers two plates behind him on the short-cut lawn, as if someone had buried a table underneath it.

It doesn't take long, and a sweet smell wafts over from the fire, even though the wind is blowing from the sea. When Friedrich Schiller sees that his guest can't identify the smell, he explains that he has soaked the meat in balsamic vinegar, honey, and oil for hours, and then sprinkled it with a pinch of cane sugar.

Thomas Mann has never tasted any of this before, and when he reaches for the plate Friedrich Schiller hands him, he notices that there is a spoon on the freshly grilled breast. When he takes it (it seems to be a kind of request), he realizes that he can easily slice the flesh with it. It's like cutting through a ripe avocado …

After the meal, Thomas Mann isn't sure where to put the plate, but Friedrich Schiller tells him to just leave it somewhere on the lawn — again, as if there were tables buried everywhere.

Meanwhile, the fire is rekindled and a pot is placed on the grate, which is still dripping with fat. The water in the pot boils within minutes—coffee is being brewed. "Cowboy coffee," as Friedrich Schiller calls it, though it soon transpires that the jet-black brew is only there to conceal large quantities of whiskey.

No matter. The tin cups are filled to the brim, a "To your health!" is exclaimed, and then Friedrich Schiller's cup collides with Thomas Mann's.

Thomas Mann doesn't know why Friedrich Schiller toasts with coffee. Maybe it's because of the whiskey, or perhaps it could be a Californian tradition he doesn't yet know—he is, after all, only a recent arrival here. But in the end it doesn't matter, because just like Friedrich Schiller he plans on staying. That's why he's building himself a house, not far from this one. He wants to spend the rest of his life up on one of the nearby hills. And now that Friedrich Schiller is sitting next to him and they have time to talk, he would like to tell him about it.

But suddenly a couple of women enter the yard, place themselves in front of the fire, and immediately take the floor. Thomas Mann doesn't know who they are or how they know his host. The only thing that's certain is that they start talking straight away, and that their words tell of Europe and the great war going on there.

Friedrich Schiller takes no notice of them. He reaches for the whiskey bottle, spurning the pot of coffee and filling his cup from it alone. Then he empties the cup with long, silent gulps.

Having done so, he places the cup on the table apparently buried in front of him and leans back and watches as the women finish their lecture, turn around, and leave the yard again. Their view to the fire is now clear once more, and perhaps this fact—along with another cup of "coffee"—is the reason why Friedrich Schiller suddenly begins to philosophize about the pointlessness of all fiction. There can be no doubt that Friedrich Schiller does not think much of the flowery fantasies of the spirit. Brilliance means nothing to him, he says, and only in the fire does he accept it.

Thomas Mann would love to object, but he isn't one of those men who seek quarrels, especially not on a stranger's farm. And so he keeps silent. He listens and his eyes wander toward a kind of copse of fir trees that grows, a little lost, in a corner of the Schiller property.

Friedrich Schiller, meanwhile, carries on talking, refilling, and reproaching, and it seems as if neither words nor whiskey could ever get him drunk.

Thomas Mann, on the other hand, feels caught in a dream from which he is unable to escape, even though he knows that he is dreaming, and only when Friedrich Schiller throws his empty tin cup on the wobbly grate and it slides over the fat and crashes into the fire, causing Schiller's stream of words to dry up for a moment, does Thomas Mann see his chance. He gets up, explains that he is tired, thanks his host for the invitation, and says goodbye. Then he hurries back home. When he arrives there, he pulls out his diary, takes his fountain pen and writes: "All very weird. A comfort to return to one's own order."

Then he goes to sleep. He will never see Friedrich Schiller again.

Friedrich Schiller is wounded by German shrapnel on a trip to Italy on May 12, 1944. Six thousand miles away, Thomas Mann is working on his novel *Doctor Faustus* that day. In the evening he plans to recite excerpts to friends and acquaintances who, like him, have fled the National Socialists and sought shelter in the hills west of Los Angeles. But something strange happens before that. As Thomas Mann walks down the street, a policeman steps up to him and forbids him to speak German in public.

That night the American author Frederick Schiller Faust succumbs to his wounds on a hill north of Naples. As a war reporter, he should have sought safety, but then he charged forward with the 88th Infantry Division's first wave of attacks and soon lay on the ground bleeding with hundreds of other men. For a while he was still breathing, and then his soul escaped through a hole in his chest. As soon as he's returned from his reading to Pacific Palisades, Thomas Mann notes in his diary: "Here the safety-first strategy and in Italy misery."

He doesn't know that Frederick Schiller Faust is no longer alive. He can't know. Faust's body isn't recovered until three days later, and the news of his death does not reach the newspapers until May 17.

On that day Thomas Mann suffers from a colic. Three weeks later he receives a painting of the dying Goethe as a birthday present.

The painting is given to him by a man named Paul Huldschinsky. He will die of stomach cancer three years later and will soon be forgotten. And even if someone decides to search for him decades later, hardly anything will be found. It is said that his estate was lost. His route to America can't be reconstructed and a photograph of him isn't anywhere to be found. Only the day of his death is known: February 1, 1947. Paul Huldschinsky dies that day at three o'clock in the morning in his house in Santa Monica, at 317 Mesa Road. Thomas Mann sends a letter of condolence. His wife attends the funeral. Eventually, I start looking for Paul Huldschinsky.

But Paul Huldschinsky isn't the only one I'm looking for. There are dozens of others who form part of the history of the house in which Thomas Mann lives. There are architects and carpenters, landscape gardeners and interior designers, builders and electricians. It is they who built the house for him on a hill west of Los Angeles and who designed the grounds with their commanding views of Pacific Ocean.

To keep the house in good condition over the years, the garden well maintained and orderly, there are also gardeners and secretaries, cooks and drivers, servants and maids.

Nobody has ever gone through their papers, hardly anyone knows how they got to America, not to mention the circumstances that brought them to the house at 1550 San Remo Drive to seek employment. Even if they make it into the house, their names usually stay outside. Many of them remain completely nameless, and even if the servants have a short appearance in Thomas Mann's diaries or in one of his letters, the staff are only afforded labels: they are an "adverse émigré domestic service couple," a "useful Negro girl," a "Danish woman," or simply "the maid."

This is a smorgasbord of abbreviations, judgements, and labels, the ABCs of the ritualized world of a man who calls himself Thomas and whose servants usually appear as quickly as they disappear, leaving behind nothing but fragments of names, professions, and ascriptions of all kinds.

There are the servants Lucy and John, Charles and Berenice, Felix and Joe, Richard and Lili; there are the domestic workers Will, Ruth, Perline, and Gussy; there's Walter's girl and a cook from Vienna, in addition to the gardener Vattaru and his wife Koto; there's a woman named Leona, and one who is only known as Olga; there's a domestic-servant couple from Texas, and the Jewish domestic-servant couple Hahn; there's old Mrs. Wallace, industrious Myrtle, and the foolish Myra; and there's a few Mexicans picking lemons, in the garden laid out by Ted Löwenstein.

Ted Löwenstein isn't an important figure in the life of Thomas Mann. No archive has collected his letters, none of his designs for the garden are preserved. No one can tell more than three lines about him, and even then it is best to use the subjunctive. We are told that "Ted Löwenstein was said to be a gardener with excellent botanical knowledge and great practical experience, who transformed the grounds around Thomas Mann's house from a completely uncultivated piece of land into a flowering garden."

This is what's recorded in the five-volume compendium of Thomas Mann's letters that enshrines the epistolary footnotes to his body of work. And although this way we learn what Ted Löwenstein, the floral caretaker, has done for Thomas Mann, the laurel bearer, the story behind it, which stretches from Germany to America to Japan, remains entirely in the dark, as unfathomable as it is unwritten.

But where to begin the search? The list of the twenty thousand letters written by Thomas Mann already comprises a total of almost four thousand pages full of names, places, and works. Ted Löwenstein is mentioned only once.

But how could it be any different? Ted Löwenstein is just a simple gardener, an earthy footnote in the life of a lofty mind, one more peripheral figure at least the name of whom, in contrast to many others, seems to be known. This is a name in which the trace of fate is lost, for Ted Löwenstein is a German Jew who emigrated to America. Unfortunately, his name cannot be found on any American naturalization list. And the passenger lists of the ships that carried all the emigrants at that time remain silent as well. Officially, a Ted Löwenstein does not exist.

The American Dream Is Slogging West, Pulling Pieces of Furniture and Whole Houses Along with It on a Rope

The story of some houses is the story of a city, the story of a country, even the story of the world. In the case of Thomas Mann, this story is well known — it has been told countless times. It is the story of how this successful author leaves his grand house in Munich's Poschingerstrasse on February 11, 1933, to give lectures on "The Sufferings and Greatness of Richard Wagner" in Amsterdam, Brussels, and Paris, but soon learns that he himself will suffer persecution and arrest by the National Socialists should he return home, which is why he decides not to and instead seeks exile for himself and his family, first in Switzerland (in Basel and Lugano), then in France (in Le Lavandou, Bandol, and Sanary-sur-Mer). At the end of 1933, they return to Switzerland, first to Zurich and then — for more than four years — to Küsnacht, from where the Mann family sets out on February 15, 1938, to travel to the French port of Cherbourg and board an ocean liner for America. They arrive in New York on February 21. Thomas Mann is immediately surrounded by reporters and declares: "Where I am, there is Germany. I carry my German culture inside me. I live in contact with the world and I don't see myself as a fallen person."

After this has been said, Thomas Mann sets out on a lecture tour of America with his head held high. From March 1 to May 6, he travels across the country and back and even throws in a small excursion to Canada.

During the following weeks, the Mann family ponders the question of where to settle. The only thing that's certain is that Mann intends to stay in America. At the end of May, the final decision is made — the university town of Princeton it will be. A villa, in keeping with his status, and a visiting professorship that is not particularly labor intensive but extremely well paid make Thomas Mann's decision easier.

Before the semester begins, however, they return to Switzerland for another two months, where the family household in exile is finally dissolved. Back in America, Thomas Mann gives four lectures at Princeton University on Goethe, Wagner, Freud, and his own work; he is awarded five honorary doctorates; and earns $6,000 in salary. Afterward, he goes on tour once more, across the country, in seven-league boots, delivering his lecture on "The Problem of Freedom." According to him, this question is essential in the face of the emerging totalitarianisms. Thomas Mann does not offer up a scholastic disputation, but rather a functional text that can easily be adapted to current developments.

The lecture tour lasts ten weeks, and Thomas Mann does not return to Princeton until April. In 1940 the tour is shortened and the lecture rewritten in view of the war that has broken out in the meantime. The summer is spent with the family in California. They have already been there for the past two summers, but this time things have changed. "Princeton bores me," explains Thomas Mann — and so their vacation plans turn into relocation plans …

The destination is the hills west of LA, and there is a good reason for this, because not only is the Pacific climate better than that of Princeton, but there is also a large local German émigré community. And it keeps growing. By the end of 1939, three hundred thousand Jewish and non-Jewish Germans have already left their homeland, and now, in 1940, another twenty thousand are joining them. It is not easy to determine how many of them are trying their luck in Los Angeles, but since America takes in a total of one hundred thirty thousand German refugees and the greater LA area has the second-largest exile community after New York, it must be tens of thousands. And thus Thomas Mann will also go to California, the topographic incarnation of the American Dream. For the time being, it is the last stage of this expulsion into paradise—and, at the same time, the first step on the way to the house whose story is told here.

And yet the story of this house is different from the one you would otherwise hear. It also begins with an escape, but one that is not politically but rather privately motivated and does not aim at leaving a country or even an entire continent. In truth, it is little more than a small expulsion within a city, from one neighborhood to another, and "expulsion" is not the right word either, because the one who is leaving does so on his own initiative. He's a free man, even if in his case that means his wife left him. Be that as it may, this man—the files are silent about his name, and all we know is that he is "some Hollywood filmmaker"—this man in any case bought a plot of land a few years ago, in the hills west of Los Angeles, at 1550 San Remo Drive, which he now, in 1940, would like to sell again, because just as his wife lost her desire for him, he lost his desire for this piece of land. So he offers it for sale—and this is the moment when a window dresser from Illinois comes into play. That is to say, a former window dresser.

His name is Frank Meline, and he arrived in Los Angeles as a young man in 1902 to live the dream they call their own in America. In Frank Meline's case, however, the dream has taken on a pretty solid form in the shape of ordinary bricks, as Frank Meline hired himself out as a construction worker before starting his own company in 1912.

The foundation stone has been laid, and the heroic story, which brings the American Dream to life in the first place, can take its course. And it does, because after Frank Meline has made enough contacts, gathered experience, and built a few conventional houses, he feels a higher calling and begins to connect the ordinary bricks with his dream. In Frank Meline's case, this means that he no longer busies himself with conventional habitations. Soon he only puts up buildings that look as if they come from another time, from another place on this earth, as if they had already had histories in foreign countries and have now decided to move to America in search of new occupants … English cottages, Spanish art nouveau chalets, French villas, Moorish palaces—whatever people ask of him, Frank Meline will build. And people in LA are asking a lot of him, not to mention those in Hollywood alone. The American Dream, on the other hand, demands only one thing from him: that he, Frank Meline, become rich. And he will.

Because his dream doesn't come to an end, but instead everyone in LA soon comes to know Frank Meline, it isn't long before the builder starts working as a broker as well, with the result that in the 1920s more than half of all houses sold in Beverly Hills are sold by him. That done and still no end in sight, Frank Meline follows the American Dream on its constant course: in addition to his construction concern, he also enters the real-estate business and in 1927 secures the sales rights for some undeveloped areas west of Los Angeles, which he gives names like "Castellammare" and the "California Riviera." The American Dream, it seems, was once at home in Europe.

Geographically, these areas belong to Pacific Palisades, a suburb of LA whose origins lie in the movie business, since the entire area once served as a huge studio area and open-air set, starting in 1911. Pacific Palisades didn't have any real inhabitants then. The only ones who lived on the more than seventeen thousand acres of land were a couple hundred cowboys and a tribe of Sioux Indians who were required for film shoots along with their cows and horses, while the principal actors lived in LA and took the tram or train out to the set in Inceville, then the world's largest movie studio.

In addition to the Indian tents and cowboy huts, Inceville also had a Swiss mountain village and a colorful collection of Japanese houses, as well as various stables, workshops, offices, a large canteen, and, down by the sea, ample space for ships and sea battles of all kinds.

Meanwhile, battles of a different kind raged up on the studio grounds, where several fires broke out over the years, and after one last major fire raged on July 4, 1922—American Independence Day—the once-mighty Inceville was nothing more than a conglomeration of charred ruins.

And yet one building survived. A small, weather-beaten church stood tall among the black rubble—and when the Methodist Church of Southern California purchased the surrounding land that same year, the twisted building must have appeared to the faithful as an apparition from another world.

The Methodists had bought about twelve hundred acres of land to make room for their community and the rapidly growing Chautauqua movement, which had been founded in 1874 in the eastern US with the aim of bringing education and culture to people all over the country—which is why, as early as 1905, President Roosevelt would call it "the most American thing in America." In the following years, more than ten thousand Chautauqua communities were established throughout the country, most of which moved from one place to another. The one in Pacific Palisades, however, was meant to be a focal point and would become the "Chautauqua of the West," two and a half thousand miles from the place where the movement had its origins.

Since the cultivation of minds can only be successful if you also cultivate the land, however, the estate acquired in Pacific Palisades was divided into lots, all kinds of roads were built, and water, electricity, and telephone pipes and cables were laid. It wasn't long before the temporary tents of the first settlers made way for pretty little houses, and by 1926 some 250 families were living in the area.

And yet, given the vastness of the country, this was not all that much, and in the northeast of Pacific Palisades there was still a large undeveloped stretch of land. It is precisely this spot for which Frank Meline acquires the building rights in 1927 and which he declares the "California Riviera" because of its geographical similarity to the one in Europe.

But Frank Meline has never seen Europe with his own eyes, and it is therefore photographs that shape his image of the Old World. Ironically, one of the most important illustrated books Meline uses as an inspiration for the piece of California that would later go down in history as "Weimar under Palmtrees" is the work of a German, Kurt Hielscher.

Hielscher, who is all but forgotten today, was a very well-known photographer in the 1920s, 1930s, and 1940s, and could, in a way, be described as the inventor of the large-format illustrated travel book. The combined print run of his works amounted to almost half a million copies. During the First World War, Hielscher was stranded in Spain, where he made a modest living as a private tutor, and between 1914 and 1919 he traveled the country with his camera, covering more than forty-five thousand kilometers and taking more than two thousand pictures. When he returned to Germany, Hielscher presented the pictures to the publisher Günther Wasmuth to discuss the possibilities for a publication. Wasmuth was based in Berlin, and while he was negotiating the publication of the pictures with Kurt Hielscher, a man whom we will meet again later moved into the former servants' quarters of the publishing house: Julius Ralph Davidson, a budding architect who had just been discharged from the German army and was looking for new challenges in his native city.

And while Davidson began to make himself at home in the attic (he did not stay long and emigrated to the United States in 1923), two

floors below Günther Wasmuth agreed to publish Hielscher's book on Spain using the rotogravure printing Hielscher had asked for. This method produced lush blacks and high-contrast greyscales, but was so expensive that it had previously been used only for the reproduction of artworks. Although Wasmuth was in financial straits, he saw Hielscher's work as a chance for a new beginning — a gamble that paid off.

In 1921 Wasmuth published *Unbekanntes Spanien* (Unknown Spain), followed in 1922 by an American edition under the title *Picturesque Spain* — a copy of which ended up with Frank Meline, who used it to shape his image of Europe.

When Meline acquires the building rights for the northeast of Pacific Palisades in 1927, it is the pictures of Spain taken by a German that determine his image of Europe and now impact on the American landscape that will become home to German and European émigrés only a few years later.

The steps taken immediately after Meline's purchase, however, are decidedly American rather than European: the quickly drawn-up zoning plans are as ingenious as they are megalomaniac, and all the newspapers hail this land seizure as a realization of the American Dream. As a result, it is not long before men, machines, and marketers arrive; the entire area is intersected by roads; and even the lousiest cul-de-sac is given a mellifluous Italian name, while the freshly divided blocks are prepared for construction and finally sold lot by lot.

A total of 386 lots are created in this way on the California Riviera alone, with San Remo Drive not even included at first, as it lies on the edge of the area and will only be developed later.

But Frank Meline doesn't care. He's got what he wants — the land.

But as it isn't enough for him to merely own the land, Frank Meline also designs the plans for some of the houses to be built on it, and it is an integral part of the story — that is, of the American Dream — that Frank Meline has neither the appropriate education nor license to work as an architect.

What Frank Meline does have is his own house, a huge villa with even bigger grounds — another part of his dream. When the first talkie version of the *Count of Monte Christo* is produced in 1934, it is shot in part on Frank Meline's estate, not least because of its vast garden, a landscape full of cypresses and palm trees, and the new villas dabbed as bright white spots between the trees, suggesting first to the film's producer, then to the camera, and finally to the rest of the world that southern France was indeed located in the hills west of Los Angeles.

In other words, Frank Meline not only has a fiction of Europe in his head and has built it in the form of streets, gardens, and houses in the hills west of LA, but — thanks to *The Count of Monte Cristo* — he also knows what it means to have had to flee from somewhere. So it's no wonder that he and Thomas Mann find each other on the orphaned property of a filmmaker. On September 12, 1940, Thomas Mann buys the one-and-a-half-acre site on San Remo Drive for $6,500. From now on, Lot 41 belongs to him.

The signature on the sales contract next to that of Thomas Mann, however, is not Frank Meline's, but that of one of his employees, a man called Clarence S. Weismann, and neither Weismann's nor Meline's names are ever mentioned in Thomas Mann's diaries or letters. And nowhere else are they recorded, not even with a single word. No one in the Thomas Mann Archive knows their names, nor has anyone in the army of Thomas Mann researchers that fills entire university auditoriums ever even referred to them. I too would never have heard of them had I not, after a series of unsuccessful attempts, at some point succeeded in deciphering the name of the company ("The Frank Meline Company") and the signature of its agent ("C. S. Weismann") on the sales contract.

These were my only leads, the loose ends of a story without which it would have been impossible to go back and find a window dresser from Illinois who would emigrate to Los Angeles, live his dream there, and, years later, on a somewhat secluded hill, meet the novelist Thomas Mann to sell him a piece of fictional riviera.

It is no longer possible to determine how Weismann came to LA and how he became part of the local property gold rush, nor what he did afterward. All that remains of him is a two-line entry in the Californian edition of the *Real Estate Directory of Brokers and Salesmen* and his data from the 1940 census. This says that Weismann was born in Iowa in 1891 and lived in LA at 51 Rose Avenue—a conventional house built in 1911 from ordinary brick.

Frank Meline, on the other hand, has to give up. He is in bad health and sells his company a year after he sells the property on San Remo Drive. He dies on August 17, 1944, in a side street of his very own dream, 331 North Rockingham Avenue.

Thomas Mann, however, stays on. And his survival is also ensured. On September 13, 1940, just one day after he buys the property, he learns that the founding of a Thomas Mann Society is planned in New York. The fact that the news reaches him on Friday the 13th doesn't bother Thomas Mann. He has become accustomed to a certain ignorance of external matters and doesn't allow himself to be distracted from his work in any other way. And so, on this day, he goes to his study at nine in the morning to write, as usual. The house—spacious, beautifully situated, and sporting a swimming pool—has only been rented by the Mann family. After all, they want to build their own house as soon as possible, and now that the land has been bought, it should only be a matter of time before it is standing in front of them. Thomas Mann is sure that they will be able to move in only a few months from now. In the meantime, they stay here at 441 North Rockingham Avenue—the very street where Frank Meline will die four years later.

But Thomas Mann won't learn anything about this, because now, in September 1940, Frank Meline still lives on his estate in Beverly Hills. And on the day they drive him away from Rockingham Avenue in a hearse, Thomas Mann will no longer be there, but will rather live in a house on a plot of land once sold to him by Frank Meline.

The day when the story reaches this little climax, however, is still a long way off, and so I have time to return to that study at 441 North Rockingham Avenue, where Thomas Mann is sitting on the morning of September 13, 1940, racking his head over a lecture while the ink on his paper runs in all directions forming all kinds of shapes but no meaningful sentences.

Admittedly Thomas Mann should have known that this would happen—after all, his mornings have always been reserved for writing literature and not for current political affairs, all the more so now that he has begun to write the final part of his novel *Joseph and His Brothers*.

But he has not been able to work on this for some days now. The lecture is an urgent matter: the first date will be soon. If the premiere goes well, he'll take it on a big American tour. The whole country, it seems, is just waiting to hear him speak about War and Democracy.

So he puts the novel aside and forces himself to compose the speech, even though his writing has resulted in little more than a set piece for days. But that's not really a big deal, after all; writing, for him, generally means nothing more than rearranging something that already exists. Seen this way, the pages can be easily filled with old ideas, and the set pieces later joined together with ink to form a whole, an opus. What better way to use ink than for covering over cracks and gaps?

This morning Thomas Mann is engaged in a mundane task, but the thought of the society bearing his name gives him a sublime sensation, at least momentarily, and a feeling of solemnity that he otherwise only experiences when people rise from their seats for a standing ovation after one of his speeches.

Meanwhile, five hundred yards to the south, at 116 North Rockingham Avenue, another man is sitting in his study as well. It is the composer Arnold Schönberg—and *he* doesn't feel like celebrating at all. He'd rather hide away. Under his desk. In his music scores. Inside a piano. Arnold Schönberg suffers from triskaidekaphobia, which means that he is afraid of the number thirteen. Today, as the thirteenth falls on a Friday, this fear increases exponentially and turns the phobia into a physical affliction. Thomas Mann knows nothing of this. He has not yet seen Schönberg in the two months that he's been here, and the last time they saw each other was two and a half years ago. Back then, in April 1938, Thomas Mann had come to Los Angeles for the first time, but his place of residence was Princeton, while his desk was still in Küsnacht, Switzerland. Now the desk is in Princeton, but Thomas Mann lives in LA.

On its eternal push toward the West, it seems, the American Dream lets pieces of furniture migrate more slowly than their owners.

But the desk was not the only thing that the Mann family was able to rescue from their Munich home, bring to Switzerland, and finally receive back in Princeton on October 7, 1938. Forty-seven boxes full of household goods had set out on the long westward journey, as well. And even if their arrival seems like a haunting to Thomas Mann, it is still better than the nothing that the majority of the emigrants brought with them.

Paul Huldschinsky knows that, too. But the son of a wealthy industrialist, who was one of the most sought-after interior designers of the Weimar Republic and lived in a summer residence on Berlin's Wannsee for many years, is spared this fate. His extensive network of friends and acquaintances includes a Hamburg shipowner, and so Paul Huldschinsky succeeds in saving the majority of his property and having his valuable furniture, expensive paintings, and library of numerous first editions shipped to America before emigrating here with his family in 1938.

What Paul Huldschinsky, on the other hand, cannot take with him to the New World is his old existence. It was not long ago that he filled the most prestigious rooms in Berlin's largest houses with splendor. As the son of an art collector, he had grown up in such rooms and frequented the most important villas in the city, and as a member of the distinguished Golf and Country Club at Wannsee, he also had the appropriate contacts to turn his renowned passion for furniture, art, and architecture into a profitable business. Paul Huldschinsky was particularly taken with furnishing magnificent libraries and the houses of art collectors, although for him it was not a problem if someone had a large mansion but no appreciation of art whatsoever, because then Paul Huldschinsky simply delivered a complete art collection as part of the furnishing. Now, however, in September 1940, he lives in the far west of Pacific Palisades, off the beaten track, at 370 Via Florence—a small street on which his is the only house—while the large villa at Tiergartenstrasse 4 in Berlin that Paul Huldschinsky had furnished a few years earlier for an art dealer is occupied by those National Socialist offices that coordinate secret euthanasia operations.

I can't say whether Paul Huldschinsky knows that the National Socialist eugenicists have seized the villa to initiate the murder of tens of thousands of physically and mentally handicapped people. What is certain, however, is that Paul Huldschinsky leaves his house in Via Florence on September 13, 1940, at 2:30 p. m. sharp. His destination is 441 Rockingham Avenue—Thomas Mann's house.

Paul Huldschinsky has known the writer for several years, having lived in Munich's Herzogpark from 1912 to 1918, not far from Poschingerstrasse, where Thomas Mann resided after 1914, and the two had met in the Residenztheater as well. And yet their closer acquaintance only arose here, in American exile, when Paul Huldschinsky attended one of Thomas Mann's lectures. Paul Huldschinsky doesn't remember exactly when that was. Maybe in March of last year. Or in April. He can't tell. What is certain is that he hadn't been in the country long when his path crossed with that of Thomas Mann for the second time. Now, a year and a half later, Paul Huldschinsky wants to make sure that their paths will cross once more, only this time he would do the talking and Thomas Mann would listen—after all, he wants to make the writer an offer.

Paul Huldschinsky drives the six miles from Via Florence to Rockingham Avenue. In America, he's grown tired of taking long walks. After all, Los Angeles is the most motorized city in the world, and the only ones still walking along the road are German émigrés who see the daily mile run as a cultural achievement to be preserved, which is partly due to the fact that many of them do not have driver's licenses. Paul Huldschinsky, on the other hand, has one, and he likes to get in the car because almost the entire route to Rockingham Avenue runs along Sunset Boulevard. And while Paul Huldschinsky leisurely chugs along and enjoys the scenery, I have time to reconstruct his journey to America. A file from New York Harbor has put me on a trail ...

The Outside World of an Interior Designer

It's as if the New World had been looking for a counterbalance, because while passenger lists of the Port of New York don't register Ted Löwenstein's entrance, they do Paul Huldschinsky's — twice.

A namesake can be ruled out. The person who lands in New York twice — on two different ships — is Paul Huldschinsky, the very same I am looking for.

Paul Huldschinsky's first arrival in America is dated November 16, 1937, his second December 5, 1938. There's 384 days between them, a voyage back to National Socialist Germany, and a stay in the Sachsenhausen concentration camp. Why Paul Huldschinsky should go to America twice isn't quite clear. What is, is that the first time around he does not intend to stay — after all, he and his wife leave their children in Germany and take only two suitcases and just a little money with them.

When Paul and Marianne Huldschinsky arrive at New York Harbor ten days after their departure from Rotterdam in November 1937, they are not alone, because Paul Huldschinsky's brother-in-law — a man named Richard George Auspitzer — is already waiting for them. He owns a house on Long Island, earns his living in America by marketing a process developed in Germany to protect iron from rust, and has a wife who works in the film industry. There is always work for interior decorators in films, Paul Huldschinsky thinks to himself.

He soon discovers, however, that his sister-in-law's job is not to furnish films, but to report on them, as she runs the subscription office of a film service. And this office isn't completely free in its judgements, but answerable to the archbishop of New York. As a result, Mrs. Auspitzer's "Motion Picture Department" doesn't publish a magazine for

VII

cineastes, but a monthly list of commendable or condemnable mov-
ies, from the standpoint of Catholic moral doctrine. Questions of
interior design are not of interest from this perspective and are only
addressed when someone lies around half-naked on an art nouveau
sofa or takes the whole Victorian "loveseat" thing a little too literally.

But as far as Paul Huldschinsky is concerned, morals aren't any his
business. Back home in Berlin, he wasn't exactly known as a blushing
flower. He liked to stay late into the night at the fashionable parties
and didn't come home even when he tired. Instead, he liked to make
himself comfortable between naked women in the apartments of his
bohemian friends and see what the rest of the night would bring.
And they brought some things, those Babylonian nights in the heart
of Berlin — for example, a visit by American dancer Josephine Baker,
who gave Paul Huldschinsky and his friends a private performance
in nothing but a small red silk apron. For hours she danced in front
of them, bending in ever new ways, and he, Paul Huldschinsky, thor-
oughly enjoyed it.

He was fond of women in many ways and made no secret of it,
which is why the art dealer Henri-Pierre Roché, who met Huldschinsky several times in the 1920s and later wrote the novel *Jules and Jim*,
modeled the figure of the rival Harold after Paul Huldschinsky — a
man of the world who loves life and women.

In his brother-in-law's house on Long Island, this world seems infinitely far away, but Paul Huldschinsky soon gets closer to it again,
at least geographically, because after less than six weeks he leaves
America to travel back to National Socialist Germany on December
23, 1937, one day before Christmas Eve. A year later, he will use the
Christmas season to travel in the opposite direction, and take a ship
from New York through the Panama Canal to Los Angeles, where he
will arrive on January 1, 1939.

But now, at the beginning of 1938, Paul Huldschinsky is back in Berlin. It seems he wants to complete a few more jobs before he finally moves to America with his wife and children. But he isn't the only one who has orders. The Nazi henchmen also have orders, and one of these is to finally apprehend Huldschinsky.

During the Kristallnacht pogrom, they bring him in. Paul Huldschinsky is arrested. He is not alone. Around thirty thousand Jews are taken into custody over the night of November 9–10. The wealthy, in particular, are targeted — they are officially referred to as "Aktionsjuden," a term that affirms the premeditated nature of the operation. Those who fall into the hands of the Berlin Gestapo are rounded up, taken to collection points, packed onto trucks, and driven to Sachsenhausen concentration camp, twenty miles away. Within a few days, the number of inmates at the camp rises from eight to over fourteen thousand.

Paul Huldschinsky is one of these. When he arrives at the camp, he is immediately robbed of his personal belongings and stripped of his clothes. His hair is shorn. Then it's on to the "bath," where the prisoners are hosed down with ice-cold water by SS officers. The new arrivals are brought to the parade ground in torn prison uniforms and have to wait for their drill, which does not commence until well after midnight. At about two o'clock in the morning, they return to the barracks, completely exhausted. Inside, there are no beds. The SS have removed them and spread out straw instead, due to the large number of prisoners.

The next morning it's an early start. The inmates are expected to labor in a nearby brickworks. Since there are no push carts, they have to use their buttoned jackets to carry the sand necessary for brickmaking to the kilns. They are also made to pull railway wagons and rollers weighing several tons. Anyone who isn't fast enough for the guards is beaten with truncheons. Those who survive the ordeal are handed an "aryanization contract," through which they agree to the surrender of their property. Sign the papers and you're out. And whoever doesn't is completely at the mercy of the guards.

Paul Huldschinsky is lucky. He is released again only twelve days later, on November 22. Or rather, he is handed over to a man named Hans Sommer, who is not only the husband of one of Paul Huldschinsky's nieces, but also a film composer so esteemed by Goebbels that he, a "half-Jew," can visit the concentration camp and retrieve Paul Huldschinsky without having to fear that he might become an inmate himself.

The very next day, Paul Huldschinsky boards a ship in Hamburg together with his wife, her daughter from her first marriage, and their own younger daughter. It is the SS *President Roosevelt*, and the destination is — once again — New York. But the number of suitcases has multiplied. And they've also taken everything else with them that was somehow transportable. This time, this much is clear: there will be no return.

During the crossing, the names of the children are Americanized. In the passenger list, Lorilott becomes Eleonore, while six-year-old Juliane becomes Juliana. Paul Huldschinsky's wife Marianne will soon call herself Mary Ann.

Paul Huldschinsky himself, however, does not change his name when, on December 10, 1938, he appears before a court on Long Island, New York, to declare his intention of becoming a citizen of the United States. When I discover the corresponding file in an archive almost eighty years later, I am astonished, because I have now not only reconstructed Paul Huldschinsky's journey to America but also — finally — found a photograph of him.

Paul Huldschinsky doesn't look particularly happy, though. He wears rimless glasses and slightly lowers his head, affecting a "what do you want from me?" look.

"Excuse me," I say, "I just want to know what happens next." Then I put the file back and hope Paul Huldschinsky will show me the way.

When Paul Huldschinsky arrives at Rockingham Avenue on September 13, 1940, shortly before six o'clock, he sees that he is not the only one who wants to speak to Thomas Mann. Two other émigrés, a young businessman from Hamburg and the doctor and writer Martin Gumpert, have also found their way to Thomas Mann. Gumpert has an eye on the famous author's daughter Erika and would like to enter into holy matrimony with her, but she stalls—and for the time being, he just sits around with her father, drinking tea and taking part in daily conversations about the war. Now, in September 1940, everything revolves around the effect of the bombs that the Royal Air Force has been dropping over German cities for over a year. A few days ago, twenty-two tons were dropped over Berlin. But the damage is said to have been small and, given the tens of thousands of leaflets dropped, the enterprise was probably more of an Allied propaganda campaign.

Paul Huldschinsky could also use a bit of propaganda—not political, but private—because business has not been going well since he moved to America. In the 1940 census, he declared that he had not received any regular income in the previous year, which is why the column indicating the number of weeks worked and the column indicating the income earned from this work both contained zeros. According to Paul Huldschinsky's own statements, in his first year in America he did still earn some money, but the files say neither how much nor how. Fortunately, his lodger, a man named Theodore Hutton, is talkative. When writes his autobiography in 1965, he casually explains: "Hulle had opened a furniture store in Beverly Hills with a former competitor from Berlin, Leni Fougner. She had a limp and was hard-working. Besides, she had money."

Paul Huldschinsky gets a small part of this money for the pictures he brought with him to America and which Leni Fougner buys from him again and again, even if it's more out of compassion than real interest. Paul Huldschinsky also makes a few dollars by selling antiques, and when he's hired to furnish director Ernst Lubitsch's living room, a bit of money comes into the coffers again.

Nevertheless, the situation is anything but rosy, because Paul Huldschinsky, who is used to upper-class living and isn't a friend of limits, lives far beyond his means, hiring two kitchen helpers and turning his house into a meeting place for exiled bohemians, which is why they not only eat well but also drink a lot of Scotch. The checks Huldschinsky writes to pay for their copious supply of alcohol from the nearby drugstore frequently bounce, but he always manages to straighten things out somehow. His visitors are always impressed and believe themselves to be in a villa on Lake Wannsee outside Berlin and not in a Californian apartment building, because of the house's old furniture and paintings. And yet behind this façade lurks financial ruin, especially since the art market is drying up after more and more works that have been branded as "degenerate" begin to appear in American auction houses and more and more paintings, prints, and engravings begin to flood the market in the wake of the numerous new arrivals.

No wonder Paul Huldschinsky takes a job in the film industry in 1940 and begins working as a set designer in one of MGM's studios. To his misfortune, he is commissioned to design gas stations there instead of prestigious rooms. The fact that American gas stations are themselves prestigious is no consolation for Paul Huldschinsky. He wants to design real rooms and furnish real houses. Rooms and houses as he furnished them before he came to America. What a happy coincidence that Thomas Mann has just bought a plot of land and wants to build a house on it …

The whole matter isn't a coincidence, because Paul Huldschinsky knows about Thomas Mann's plans. Two days ago, when he had dinner with his wife and children at the Mann residence, building the house was already the dominant topic, but nothing had been decided at that time. Now that the land has been bought and construction is to commence as soon as possible, Paul Huldschinsky believes that the time has come to present his wish to the future landlord. He says he would like to take over the interior design of the house on San Remo Drive.

Thomas Mann doesn't really know what to say to this. The idea sounds tempting, but in view of Huldschinsky's previous work it doesn't sound cheap — and his wife Katia is in charge of financial matters. He himself doesn't even know where money is kept. Once, when she wasn't around and he was alone in the house, the man from the dry cleaners came to deliver his suit and tried to collect payment. But Thomas Mann had no cash on him and also no idea where to find any in the house, so the laundry man left — and took the suit with him.

But Paul Huldschinsky is lucky. Instead of having to leave empty-handed, Katia Mann steps into their cozy circle — and Paul Huldschinsky presents his wish a second time. It would be, he says, a great honor for him to be able to furnish her future home. Katia Mann reflects for a moment — in her mind's eye the old homeland emerges, she sees the venerable houses and the prestigious rooms that Paul Huldschinsky has furnished — and says, "Dear Paul, I have all the confidence in you, but we simply could not afford it." Paul Huldschinsky is prepared. He expected such an answer and has prepared his own in return. "I would take almost nothing for it at all, just the coverage of the expenses," he says. "If everyone in Hollywood sees that I have furnished Thomas Mann's house — that would be very useful to me, that would make my reputation."

"But of course you should do it, then," says Katia, and Thomas Mann nods in approval. He's really glad his wife takes care of the money.

Architecture Competitions Are Decided
at Cocktail Parties
(At Least, I Suppose They Are)

On September 18, 1940, it's all about to start. Thomas Mann has hired the architect Paul László and takes him on a tour of the property on San Remo Drive. László was born in Hungary in February 1900 and enrolled as a student in Vienna. From the late 1920s onward, he established a reputation as an architect, especially in the South of Germany. He made it into the tea room of Hitler's Eagle's Nest with the furniture he designed, though he himself was not aware of this, nor was Hitler, who was more interested in beer halls than tea rooms — and when the construction of the Eagle's Nest began and the furniture he had designed was installed there in 1937, the Jew Paul László had already found refuge from persecution in America.

There is no way of knowing when and how Thomas Mann became aware of Paul László, but László had excellent contacts in the Californian émigré community. He built his first residence in Pacific Palisades in the summer of 1940, and once published a series of articles on upper-middle-class lifestyle culture in the German magazine *Mein Heim, Mein Stolz* (My home, my pride), which described his designs as having been "composed in creative intellectuality" and called their creator an artist. Reason enough for Thomas Mann to leave his study on North Rockingham Avenue for a moment, get into Paul László's car, and take him to San Remo Drive ...

A few thousand feet above, the photographer Eugene Swarzwald soars through the Californian sky. Once again, he is on a great exploratory mission through his beloved American West, photographing whatever appears beneath him. When he circles over San Remo Drive shortly after one p.m., Thomas Mann is already gone. Immediately

VIII

after viewing the site, the writer hurried back home to dictate the war-and-democracy lecture to his secretary on her typewriter, and Paul László disappeared again. From his flying machine, Eugene Swarzwald, therefore, glimpses only dusty roads and a patch of land divided into multiple lots, with neither people nor houses on them, and the only thing that reminds him of California are the lemon trees, thousands of which stand around on the still-undeveloped lots.

Paul László doesn't think much of hanging about. He's a man who goes straight to the heart of matters. When he emigrated to America in 1936, he bought a car on his arrival day in New York and drove it straight to LA—stopping only for two meals, three bathroom breaks, and four fuel stops. And because he likes luxury just as much as immediacy, he parked his car in classy Beverly Hills, took up residence there on the spot, and no longer ate his meals in roadside diners but in the trendy Brown Derby restaurant, just a stone's throw from his new studio on Rodeo Drive. When he drives his car to Rockingham Avenue on September 26, only eight days after the site inspection, he has already completed the first building plans for the house, which is why on this day Thomas Mann has his five o'clock tea with his usual spoonful of sugar as well as several drawings. As Katia Mann is sitting at the table with them, Paul László can also present the calculations right away. The house would cost $22,000, $16,000 of which would be covered by a mortgage.

That's a considerable sum of money, but the plans are very promising, and Thomas Mann is particularly taken by the study with its large terrace. The fact that on that very day a pipe had burst in 441 Rockingham Avenue and Thomas Mann couldn't take a hot bath, and is therefore in a bad mood, helps to ease his decision in favor of the new house. His wife Katia can't sway him, even though $22,000 is a lot of money. When it comes to temperament, this she knows: her sensitive husband is stubborn.

But Thomas Mann's mood doesn't improve the next day, as he suffers the oppressive heat. Outside he gets a headache walking along the boardwalk, and inside he has to deal with letters from people who are either asking for help or expressing their condolences because his son-in-law Jenö Lányi has died.

Together with his wife Monika and more than four hundred other souls, including ninety children who were part of a British-government evacuation program, Lányi had boarded a steamer in Liverpool to flee England, which was threatened by German bombs. The SS *City of Benares* was bound for Canada, but it never got there. On September 18, exactly one minute after midnight, a German submarine discovered the ship in the North Atlantic no-man's-land somewhere between Ireland, Iceland, and Greenland—ploughing through heavy seas at wind force five. It was attacked with torpedoes and sank within thirty minutes. Jenö Lányi drowned, while Monika Mann was rescued from the waves.

Thomas Mann records the "torpedoing of an English children's ship" in his diary on September 22, unaware that his own daughter and her husband had been on board. And even one day later, when more and more details about the fate of the ship are filtering through, Thomas Mann does not associate the incident with his daughter and her husband and merely notes that the well-known publicist and lawyer Rudolf Olden died in the attack.

On the morning of September 24, however, he receives a telegram from his daughter Erika, who is working as a war correspondent for the BBC in London. She informs him that Monika was also aboard the ship, but fortunately survived the attack and is now in a hospital somewhere in Scotland. Thomas Mann does not learn much more, and even three days later, on September 27, he still has no information on Monika's condition, and the only thing he really knows is the situation on Rockingham Avenue.

"Lack of water," Thomas Mann notes in his diary that day, and it is not entirely clear whether it's a grotesque irony of history, his own lack of sensitivity to interpersonal issues, or simple thoughtlessness that leads him to repeatedly lament the "water calamities" in his house during those days just after his son-in-law had drowned in the North Atlantic and his own daughter was adrift in a lifeboat for twenty hours before she was rescued by a British vessel.

What is clear, however, is the date of Paul László's next visit: he will pass by North Rockingham Avenue again on September 27, this time not to take his prominent client to the construction site, but to pick him up and show him around one of the other houses he has designed. Lázló assumes that once Thomas Mann has seen an example of his work, he won't withdraw the commission. And so he takes him to Bel Air, to the Rosenson House, an extremely presentable villa that has just made it onto the cover of *California Arts & Architecture* magazine.

The viewing goes well — until Paul László mentions the price of the Rosenson House. "$24,000," he says, which makes Thomas Mann suspicious, because the Rosenson House is smaller than the one that László intends to build for him for what he says will be $22,000. Which raises the question: How can a larger house cost less?

When the architect is confronted with this conundrum, he does not have an answer, and Thomas Mann concludes that his own house cannot realistically come in at $22,000 — especially since Paul László is neither fond of compromise nor a fan of social housing. The house at San Remo Drive will require $22,000 plus *x*, and this *x* won't be insubstantial. Thomas Mann can do nothing but put on a brave face as the sight of a strange villa in Bel Air exposes his own house as a pipe dream.

As soon as Paul László has dropped him off at home, Thomas Mann confides in his diary that "it appears that our desires are not to be reconciled with our financial readiness."

What is to be done then? Thomas Mann doesn't know. He is depressed, sobered, and beset by doubts — and the news from Europe only makes everything worse.
"Our friends are dying. The wasteland grows," he notes, waiting not only for news from his daughter Monika but also from his son Golo and his brother Heinrich. As Thomas Mann has learned by now, they were able to escape from occupied France in a daring getaway across the Pyrenees to Spain and Portugal. Now they are stuck in Lisbon, this huge anteroom on the edge of a Europe that is burning from its center outward in all directions, hoping to catch a ship to America. Meanwhile, Thomas Mann is sitting in his rented house on Rockingham Avenue and doesn't know how to build his own. On September 29, he drives to San Remo Drive with a few acquaintances in order, as he writes, "to have the grounds admired." Two days later, the accompanying dwelling finally materializes. Paul László is back. He has designed a more economical version of the villa, but Thomas Mann doesn't like it.

There seems to be no point in spending any more time on scaled-down architecture, and the agreed lease period for the house on Rockingham Avenue has also expired. Thomas Mann must return to Princeton. He knows that there will be no progress on the San Remo Drive property until further notice, and when Paul László leaves the yard by car, this chapter is closed for the time being. It is the last mention of Paul László in his diary and their paths will never cross again.

Instead, another architect enters the scene — or at least someone who pretends to be one. On October 5, as Thomas Mann has just started packing his things for his return to Princeton, Frank Meline shows up at his door. He has heard about the problems with the architect László and quickly created his own design. This should be the perfect moment for a big hallelujah, a huge hooray resounding all the way from Rockingham Avenue to San Remo Drive. But unfortunately, Frank Meline's plan is not what Thomas Mann imagines for his Californian villa. So he bids the contractor—and his American dream house—farewell, and leaves for the East Coast.

A week later, on October 13, Thomas Mann is back in his Princeton villa. He describes a sense of homecoming. On the same day, his son Golo and his brother Heinrich arrive in New York by ship. A few days later Thomas Mann's eldest daughter Erika arrives. On October 28, she is followed by Monika. Finally, the Mann family is reunited.

Meanwhile, on the other side of the country, two and a half thousand miles to the west, the *Los Angeles Times* publishes a short article. The headline reads, "Thomas Mann Buys in Riviera District." What follows is a brief description of the plot and the poet, followed by the words: "Plans for a large residence are being prepared."

Do the journalists know something the records haven't revealed? Or are they just a little behind the times? At first glance, the latter seems more likely, since Thomas Mann is still in Princeton on January 4, 1941, and there is nothing to suggest that there will soon be a house on his Californian property.

Having spent the morning of January 4 writing, as usual, Thomas Mann is chauffeured by his butler to one of the exclusive residential areas just outside Princeton for a walk before lunch. After the meal he rests for an hour, then at five o'clock he has his tea and finally opens the daily mail. And yet this time it is a bit different because between all the letters, petitions, and pamphlets, he comes across an envelope that piques his interest. Thomas Mann pulls it out, reaches for the large ivory knife that serves as his letter opener, and opens the envelope with a clean cut. Shortly afterward, he notes in his diary: "New building plans from the architect Davidson, attractive enough to excite us again about the idea of building and settling."

Were these plans already in the works in October, and did the *Los Angeles Times* know about them? Maybe, maybe not. Who knows where a story that takes place between two coasts begins and ends? The only thing that's certain is that the architect Julius Ralph Davidson appears in Thomas Mann's paper trail for the first time on January 4, 1941. How he came to draw up building plans for Thomas Mann, I don't know. I can't say for sure how they even found each other. Neither in Thomas Mann's diaries nor his letters is there any hint, and that repository of history commonly called "secondary literature" contains only hearsay.

One source claims that the director Ernst Lubitsch introduced the architect to the writer, while others believe that contact with Davidson was established via the art dealer Galka Scheyer, who had also emigrated to America in the early 1920s and had met Davidson there, in the Hollywood home of architect Rudolf Schindler, who in turn knew Paul László, who in turn knew Thomas Mann … But let's not go there.

Whatever way you look at it, the whole matter is rather confusing, and there is no avenue of serious research that clarifies how the writer Thomas Mann came into contact with the architect Julius Ralph Davidson, especially since no source cites any real evidence for any claims made. But I am fortunate enough to be able to draw on the *Los Angeles Times*. And the *Times* could draw on a resourceful society reporter. And that society reporter had a vested interest in chronicling her own exploits, especially when it came to celebrity cocktail parties in plush settings.

And thus on the morning of October 3, 1939, she wrote about a party she had attended the night before at the exclusive Town House Hotel in Los Angeles: "Dr. and Mrs. Hans Schaeffer of New York City and Paul Huldschinsky entertained with a cocktail party and exhibit of old paintings at the Town House. One of the outstanding paintings was Rembrandt's *Portrait of an Officer*. Among the art enthusiasts attending were Mr. and Mrs. Walter Camp Jr., Mr. and Mrs. J. R. Davidson, Mrs. Edward G. Robinson, Mrs. Ira Gershwin, and Mr. Max Reinhardt."

Admittedly, this isn't conclusive proof, but it's good enough for a lucky researcher's hypothesis: perhaps it was Paul Huldschinsky who connected with Davidson and referred him to Thomas Mann.

I cannot say why Davidson only comes into play after both László and Meline are out of the picture. But maybe, like so many big stories, this little one is based on banalities. Maybe in September 1940 Davidson was simply too busy to offer his services or to be brought into play by God-knows-who, when it came to designing Thomas Mann's house, since at that time he had to finish the building plans for an entire apartment complex and a series of houses in LA—with follow-up projects already lined up (a beach house here, a villa there …).

But perhaps Davidson, who is known to be somewhat reserved, simply did not want to impose himself, at least not in the manner of his fellow architect Richard Neutra. Neutra was definitely keen to design a house for Thomas Mann, which is why he called the writer in California as early as April 1938—long before Paul László's efforts to persuade him—in order to tell him that he should stay away from mediocre architects and pick the best in the field: i.e., him, Richard Neutra.

The fact that Thomas Mann was only vacationing in the area at that time and had no plans to move to California, nor indeed any suitable property there, did not bother Richard Neutra in the least. He simply stopped by, invited Thomas Mann and both their wives into his car, and drove with this illustrious party from one modernist villa to the next. And because the whole thing was supposed to make an impression, Richard Neutra stopped from time to time, rang the bell and, when the doors were opened, shouted, "I'm the architect, let me through!," before showing off the interiors to the baffled company.

The whole thing was "unpleasant," Thomas Mann noted in his diary that evening, especially since the houses he visited did not appeal to him at all. They didn't resemble cozy homes so much as glass cubes that people with too much money and too little taste had scattered all over the area. But it seems Thomas Mann didn't say anything to Richard Neutra. At least not loudly enough, because shortly afterward Neutra showed up again, this time at a party, where he pestered Thomas Mann with his plans until it got too much and Mann eventually struck back — with words only, of course, as was his way. "Get that Neutra off my back!," he exclaimed — and with that Richard Neutra was out of the game before it had even started properly.

But now, in January 1941, the game has reopened, and the candidate Davidson has a good chance to win the architectural auction, even though he is not officially registered as an architect at all, only as an "architectural designer." Whatever. After the Mann family has dissolved their household in Princeton, found suitable temporary accommodation in Pacific Palisades, and moved to LA on March 26, the time has come — and just a few hours later Thomas Mann and the architect Davidson are sitting around a table. As usual, Thomas Mann's wife Katia has organized the meeting and made all the necessary arrangements. But there is another man sitting with them at the table, and no one knows exactly where he comes from ...

IX

Ernst Moritz Schlesinger is a handsome fellow. On the evening of March 26, 1941, he sits together with Julius Ralph Davidson, Thomas Mann, and his wife Katia in the bar of the luxurious Ambassador Hotel and drinks hot chocolate. Hotels like the Ambassador are not really in his budget, but if everything goes well they could be, because then he will have hit the jackpot — five years after leaving Germany and seeking exile in America. Five years that were anything but easy for him …

It is July 25, 1936, when Ernst Moritz Schlesinger, a merchant from Berlin, and his wife, Margarete, board the trading vessel the SS *Oregon* in Le Havre, France. Four weeks later, after the ship has crossed the Atlantic, pushed its bulk of six thousand gross-register tons through the Panama Canal, and made stops in Nicaragua, El Salvador, and Guatemala, it moors in the port of Los Angeles — and Ernst Schlesinger steps onto American soil.

He has visited the country once before, in 1927, but at that time he only stayed for two months and then travelled back to Berlin. But now, in August 1936, he is barred from returning to Germany because his passport contains the word "Hebrew."

The only problem is that Ernst Schlesinger can't simply stay in America, since he only has a visitor's visa which expires after three months. He owes getting the visa at all to his brother Paul, who came to America two years prior and now lives in Beverly Hills, where he earns his living as a real-estate agent. As such, he can offer shelter to his brother and his wife, but when the visa expires, he can't do anything more for them, and at the end of November 1936 Ernst and Margarete Schlesinger leave Los Angeles and head south. Their destination is the Mexican border town of Mexicali.

When they arrive there, they immediately go to the American consulate and apply for a visa that guarantees them permanent residence in the United States. Since the number of German emigrants
seeking exile in America is comparatively low at this time, and the
annual quota of twenty-five thousand has not yet been reached, the
Schlesinger couple is granted the coveted permit after just two days,
and is back in Beverly Hills on December 12. Less than ten weeks
later, on February 17, 1937, Ernst Schlesinger submits his application to become a citizen of the United States. After that, I lose track
of him.

When I rediscover Ernst Schlesinger in the census files of 1940, he
is living in the northwest of the city and claims to be a contractor.
Yet, if his file is accurate, he has not received a single contract over
the past year and consequently not earned a single dollar as a contractor. How then, I ask myself, does Schlesinger make a living? How
has he kept his head above water all these years? The census data
only states that he works forty hours a week. That's all I can discover,
and, as so often, it takes chance and aimlessness to find what I'm
looking for.

Weeks later, when I leaf through some files of the Emergency Rescue
Committee, the aid organization that helped numerous intellectuals
and artists escape from occupied France to the United States between
1940 and 1942, I come across a telegram signed "Schlesinger." It was
sent from Los Angeles on September 28, 1940, to the exiled writer
Hermann Kesten, who lives in New York. The telegram states that he,
Schlesinger, is a simple laborer who earns so little that he does not
even pay income tax.

There is nothing more in the telegram, but it is interesting that Kesten should be the recipient, since he is one of two "honorary advisers"
to the Emergency Rescue Committee—along with Thomas Mann,

with whom he engages in a lively correspondence at the time—and as such is decisively involved in the issue of emergency visas for those most threatened by the Hitler regime and its henchmen. Since Schlesinger is already in America, however, there must be another reason for the message, and when I see that someone has written the word "Spiro" in pencil under the telegram, I begin to expand my investigation. I am not alone, though. A librarian helps me to search the committee's files, and it doesn't take long before we come across a further document.

It's a letter dated September 10, 1940. The sender is the director of a Bank of America branch office located in Santa Monica—and the recipient is no less than the American consul in Paris.

According to the bank director, he is writing this letter at Ernst Schlesinger's request, to state that Ernst Schlesinger is a customer of his bank and as such intends to sponsor the emigration to America of a certain Eugen Spiro and his wife, Elisabeth.

The bank director confirms that although Mr. Schlesinger's account balance has averaged only small, three-figure sums over the past four years, he is a man of good character and should be relied upon to meet any obligation since he owns a share in a piece of land in Los Angeles worth $20,000. So Ernst Schlesinger is not as penniless as he stated in his census file, and when the official affidavit of support that Schlesinger filed for Eugen Spiro and his wife turns up a little later, I see that his share of the property earns him an annual $1,200 in rental income.

I don't know where Schlesinger got the land from, only that it is situated right in the heart of LA, at 108 Sycamore Avenue, and that Ernst Schlesinger and his brother Paul are the owners—since at least 1937, because there is a tax bill from that year.

In essence, this says it all, as everyone knows that tax bills are the end of all fictions. And I had painted such a beautiful picture of Ernst Schlesinger … He, a destitute emigrant, who comes to America, lives from hand to mouth as a building contractor for years, finally encounters Thomas Mann, and wins the lottery by building him a house … Unfortunately, this story is a little too good to be true. Because not only does Ernst Schlesinger receive $1,200 a year from rental payments and, on top of that, have a few hundred dollars in the bank, according to all I have learned, he also earns another $40 a week with various jobs as a handyman. When you consider that an average weekly income in 1940 is only $26, this isn't a bad living.

Sure, it still doesn't elevate him to the level of the Ambassador Hotel. This exclusive establishment is not only frequented by presidents and the rich and famous of show business, but also hosts the annual Academy Awards ceremony. And yet the fact that he, Ernst Schlesinger, the businessman from Berlin who came to this country less than five years ago, sits at the bar of the Ambassador Hotel on the evening of March 26, 1941, talking to Thomas Mann, his wife Katia, and the architect Julius Ralph Davidson about the construction of a house on San Remo Drive is an indication that he is headed in the right direction. More precisely, they sit at the bar of Cocoanut Grove, the famous nightclub that is the secret heart of the extravagant hotel. In 1926, Davidson completely redesigned its interior. But he's not the only one who has a connection to this place. Thomas Mann's former neighbor, the composer Arnold Schönberg, has also been here before, the world premiere of his work *Kol Nidre* having taken place in the club in October 1938.

However, while Arnold Schönberg still lives on North Rockingham Avenue in March 1941 and will not move away, Thomas Mann has found a new home in LA. It's not really a home at all, only a provisional stopover before he can have the lemon trees at 1550 San Remo Drive cleared and put down roots there himself.

On April 8, 1941, Thomas Mann moves into his "bus shelter" in Pacific Palisades at 740 Amalfi Drive. This stopgap has a white exterior, a clean interior, and a rural location. It is only a mile and a half, as the crow flies, to the San Remo Drive construction site — just a walk up the hill and you're on the lot.

At least in theory. Things are a little different in practice, and while it's cold and rainy outside, Katia Mann turns on the heating in the house. And since the chill lingers, the rain continues for days, and Thomas Mann has to do without his usual walks, the underheated bus shelter soon turns into a den of overwrought ruminations. Thomas Mann doubts more or less everything and everyone: his work (the accursed *Joseph* novel!), his health (that dreadful tooth!), the world as a whole (this bellicose delusion!), and certainly the folly of home-building (the ever-expanding cost!).

The architect Davidson has estimated $30,000 for the house, but because of rapidly rising prices and an increasingly uncertain financial situation for the Mann family, this is at least $10,000 too much — and for this reason, Davidson is sitting at their table again on April 15.

This time, they do not meet in the luxurious Ambassador Hotel, but in the inadequately furnished kitchen of the Amalfi Drive stopgap. The conversation revolves around the question of whether the existing design could be reduced in size or whether a new one should be made.

Three days later Thomas Mann and his wife Katia make a decision at the breakfast table. The house will neither be downsized nor redesigned; it won't ever be built in the first place.

For Thomas Mann, this withdrawal is liberating. He goes to see Davidson to tell him that he will be paid for his services, then invites Huldschinsky for tea and explains the situation to him as well, only to be informed by his wife the following day that everything is completely different now — in other words, the withdrawal has been withdrawn.

Their daughter Erika has called and announced that there is an architect who will design the house for free. His name is Paul Lester Wiener, and he knows the Mann family quite well since he recently published an essay on "New Trends in Architecture" in Klaus Mann's magazine *Decision*. Besides, he is the son-in-law of Henry Morgenthau, the US secretary of the Treasury, and you never know what such a connection might be good for. It's never bad to have friends in high places, although in this case, it is, of course, a place of their own that is the main prize.

Or rather, *could* be the main prize, because although Erika Mann recommends Paul Lester Wiener's services, Thomas Mann sees the offer as a "new perspective" and Klaus Mann informs his mother by letter, "I want to talk to Wiener about your house right away." Nothing happens. The name Paul Lester Wiener does not appear again either in Thomas Mann's letters nor in his diaries. But Erika, who brought Wiener into play, writes to her father a few days later telling him to call the whole thing off because she questions whether "this good architect, who is somehow spoiled by wealthy clients, will be able to design what is essentially just a glorified cabin."

Thomas Mann is beginning to have doubts. The second-rate stopgap on Amalfi Drive soon witnesses a new round of first-rate ruminations. Stay or go? East or west? Bury the plans or finally build the abode?

This goes on for weeks, from April to May to June. When inflation finally reaches new heights, prices keep climbing, and workers and supplies are hard to come by; when Thomas Mann's American patron Agnes Meyer advises him not to build a house and Katia Mann considers the dissolution of the Princeton household, and their entire move to the West Coast, to be "unforgivable hubris"; and when Thomas Mann is extremely unhappy about the situation, the decision is finally made.

1550 San Remo Drive will be built. A house with twenty rooms, no more. Built according to designs by Davidson, whose plan relates the circuitous route to the final decision with utmost brevity: "Plan February 28, 1941. Revised March 29, April 14, May 15."

Maybe the definite is nothing more than an accumulation of the random. If so, it must have been fate — or maybe it was just a deep longing to finally live under one's own roof again, to work and to present oneself and an entire culture — that swayed the "persistent villa owner" Thomas Mann to go ahead and build the house after all.

Or maybe the reason can be found in Thomas Mann's apathy, his temperamental mixture of contempt and trust, regardless of good advice or extraneous developments.

But perhaps the fact that they had come too far, and that not building would now be almost as expensive as building, also played a role. Or was the decision due to the guarantee of his patron Agnes Meyer, which allowed Thomas Mann to come to the conclusion "I don't need to worry about money"? Or all of the above? Who knows …

What is sure is that Katia and Thomas Mann sign a contract with Ernst Schlesinger for the construction of the house on June 21, 1941. Planned costs amount to $24,000.

The very same day Thomas Mann rejects the possibility of building a house under the given circumstances.

In Germany, final preparations are made for the war against the Soviet Union that will begin the following day.

The architecture of the entire world balances on a knife's edge. That of the house hangs in the balance.

Now things can take their course.

Pictures of California

On the day of the groundbreaking ceremony, Thomas Mann has his servant John drive him to the construction site. When he arrives on the property at San Remo Drive, a handful of journalists are already waiting for him, but Thomas Mann is not at all in the mood for the impending ceremony. He would rather sit on the chaise longue in his study and continue reading Goethe's *Good Wives*. Or lie in bed and take a siesta. This would be ideal, as he has been feeling worn out and listless for several days now, which is why he had his blood drawn in the hospital this morning, though this has only increased the emptiness within him. Moreover, his family doctor, Doctor Wolff, has put him on medication for his constant intestinal complaints, the "excessive effect" of which has meant that Thomas Mann's gut flora is just like an army in the war: from the moment it's deployed, it's up shit creek.

So it goes. It's Monday, July 7, 1941, twelve noon on the dot. On the construction site, Thomas Mann knows he has to give the assembled journalists some soundbite.

"I'm going to be a real Californian now," he says, pointing to the lemon trees all over the property. He can't imagine that in a few months the poet Bertolt Brecht will arrive in the area and scan all the lemon trees in California for price tags.

But fortunately Brecht isn't here yet, and Thomas Mann is the center of journalistic attention until further notice. "It's a nice feeling to have a little place you can call your own," he says, referring to the acre and a half of land that surrounds him. It seems that Thomas Mann has already adjusted his notions of scale to his new homeland and views his property through the eyes of an American.
The reporters record his remarks on their notepads.

When they are finished, Thomas Mann's wife Katia takes the floor and explains that here in California there are people who marry, start building houses, and divorce before they're even finished.

The reporters are holding on to their notepads.

The photographer in attendance refrains from commenting and silently takes his pictures.

Thomas Mann considers the photos unnecessary.

Paul Huldschinsky considers it unnecessary to be photographed.

Schlesinger and Davidson bear it and are thus included in the pictures. They are holding up a two-meter-long building plan, while Thomas Mann stands between them and contemplates the house that is about to jump from the page and rise in front of him—with two floors and 4,300 square feet of living space, it is not exactly what one might call a "modest" abode.

A few hundred meters above, Eugene Swarzwald soars through the Californian sky. He is still on a great exploratory mission through his beloved American West, capturing the land beneath him as it is beginning to be transformed. When he circles over San Remo Drive shortly after one p. m., Thomas Mann is already on his way again. Once his speech was finished and the building plan refolded, he got back into the car and had John drive him down to the promenade for a walk. The journalists have disappeared as well. From his flying machine, Eugene Swarzwald can see nothing but the familiar dusty roads, but on the lots in between them there have been quite a few changes. In many parts of the California Riviera, houses have been erected and driveways, garages, and gardens have been built. San Remo Drive is still empty, but Eugene Swarzwald sees a big cloud of smoke rising a little further south on one of the construction sites. It appears someone is burning lemon trees on his property.

When Eugene Swarzwald finishes his reconnaissance mission, he turns around and flies further west. He will learn soon enough about what had happened below him on 1550 San Remo Drive. The picture, which all the newspapers will print over the next few days next to their reports from the groundbreaking ceremony, was taken by a photographer from the Pacific Press—of which he, Eugene Swarzwald, is the owner.

He owns much more than that, such as a large photo agency, an even larger collection of images, and a magazine called *Pictorial California and the Pacific*, which is not only read by millions of people but also sent to hotels, travel agencies, and bus companies throughout the country as part of official advertising campaigns. It is, therefore, Eugene Swarzwald who, with his various enterprises, has not only captured the groundbreaking ceremony for Thomas Mann's house but will also shape the image of California, as well as that of the entire American West, for decades to come.

Swarzwald himself, however, is completely forgotten. So much so that the archivist who keeps his papers is not even able to tell me when he died. At some point, it seems, he simply left, and all he left behind is his American Dream, which has been slumbering in a Californian archive for decades, packed in fifty-five boxes.

Thomas Mann, on the other hand, continues to be the subject of newspaper coverage, and after the *Los Angeles Times* reports on the groundbreaking ceremony on July 12, the West Coast edition of the émigré journal *Aufbau* informs its readers, on August 15, about Thomas Mann's future home. "The villa offers the poet a panoramic view of the Pacific Ocean from his study, and will bear the name 'Seven Palms' after a group of tall palm trees," *Aufbau* reports.

The accompanying picture, however, shows nothing but lemon trees in the background behind Thomas and Katia Mann, who are looking at the building plans together with Davidson and Schlesinger.

The plume of smoke captured in Eugene Swarzwald's photographs is nowhere to be seen. Neither is Ted Löwenstein. Unlike Paul Huldschinsky, however, Löwenstein didn't sneak out of the picture, because the gardener wasn't even present at the ceremony. He first shows up on the site five weeks later. No one knows how he got there. And the few who mention Ted Löwenstein at all only say: "Ted Löwenstein came from Germany and built a garden for Thomas Mann in California. That's all we know about Ted Löwenstein."

But it's not that easy — neither for Ted Löwenstein, who is conspicuously absent at the groundbreaking ceremony, nor for me, as I still have no idea who this Ted Löwenstein really is, where he came from, and why there aren't any records of his arrival in America, as exist for everyone else in this story. Not to mention the questions of when and where he met Thomas Mann in the first place, and how it came to be that he is standing beside him on the construction site on August 14, 1941, to map out the garden.

If You're Looking for a Gardener, You're Allowed to Bark Up the Wrong Tree Occasionally

It's quite simple: If you don't have a name yet, in America you can make one for yourself with a little luck and skill, and if you have only a small name, you can discard it easily and give yourself a new one. One that fits in with America. One you can go places with.

This is only a thought, but it helps me to ignore the "Ted," given the archival vagaries I encounter in my search for Ted Löwenstein, and to limit my research to the name "Löwenstein" for the time being, in the hope that I have overlooked something. What I must not overlook, however, is the fact that "Löwenstein" is occasionally also spelled "Loewenstein" and that—given the lack of umlauts used by the American passport authorities—the corresponding person could also be called "Lowenstein."

There are hundreds of Löwen-, Loewen-, and Lowensteins who emigrated to America in the 1930s—and all of them came by boat. So I dive back into the passenger lists one more time. When I find the file of a certain Joseph Löwenstein after several days of searching, I don't suspect anything. But then I read his application for naturalization—and under the heading "occupation," it says "landscape gardener." It seems I found Thomas Mann's gardener.

At least the data matches. On March 3, 1934, Joseph Löwenstein boards a ship in Bremen to travel to Los Angeles. He is thirty-three years old, has neither wife nor children, is Jewish and was born in Battenfeld, in northern Hesse. I am not bothered by the fact that he is registered as a "commercial employee" on the passenger list of the SS *Seattle*. The journey to California takes enough time to change not only one's name but also one's profession.

One month later, on April 4, 1934, Joseph Löwenstein disembarks in Los Angeles as Josef Loewenstein and shortly after moves into lodgings at 978 ½ Fedora Street, right in the middle of downtown LA. There aren't any gardens to be seen here, and even the nearest park is more than a mile away. But it doesn't matter. Josef Loewenstein will adjust to the situation in America and adopt a new name five years later. On October 31, 1939, the day of his naturalization, Josef Loewenstein applies for permission to change his name to Josef Walter Lowry. The request is granted — and I can start looking for traces of a man with that name, traces that will eventually take me to the garden of the property on San Remo Drive.

It doesn't take long for the story to begin to unfold before me.
Joseph Löwenstein as a young man in uniform, 1917.
Joseph Löwenstein's birth certificate, a certified copy from 1939, with a swastika stamp on it and the English note "Copy Birth Certificate" written in pencil next to it.
Josef Loewenstein's entry in the 1940 census.
Josef Walter Lowry's family tree in a genealogical database.

When I contact the person who created the family tree, I learn that I've followed the wrong man.

From: Francis Nenik
To: Julie Dock
04.21.2017

Dear Julie Dock,
My name is Francis Nenik and I'm a German novelist. At the moment, I'm working on a book about a house in Pacific Palisades, Los Angeles. Thomas Mann, the German writer, and winner of the Nobel Prize in Literature, lived there from 1942–1952. In 1941/42 Josef Loewenstein created the garden of this house. Therefore I'm

looking for any kind of information about Mr. Loewenstein (later Josef Walter Lowry). While searching a genealogical database, I found pictures of him and his family as well as his birth certificate on your profile. My question is: Do you have any more information or documents about Josef Loewenstein?

With kind regards,
Francis Nenik

From: Julie Dock
To: Francis Nenik
04.22.2017

Dear Mr. Nenik,
I was delighted to receive your letter inquiring about Josef Lowenstein, and I have much information to give you. First of all, Joseph was not the landscape gardener who worked on Thomas Mann's property. That was his younger brother Theodore Lowenstein, my maternal grandfather …

What do you want me to say? If you fail to see that the only plausible resolution of "Ted" is Theodor and not Joseph, you're bound to bark up one wrong tree after another instead of finding the gardener.

It's just a thought, but it helps me to make a U-turn in the cul-de-sac I've been researching myself into and to tell the story anew.

On January 14, 1931, Theodor Löwenstein boards a ship in Bremen to sail for New York. According to the passenger list, he is twenty-eight years old, married, Jewish, and was born in Battenfeld, in northern Hesse. I am not concerned that he is identified as a "gardener" on the passenger list, because somewhere along the way someone crosses out that title and writes "skilled agriculturist" in its place.

It seems that on the journey to America, it is not only names that are adapted to the local linguistic possibilities—professions are also adapted to the vastness of the country.

On January 21, 1931, Theodor Löwenstein disembarks as Theodore Lowenstein in New York. He's alone. His wife and daughter have stayed in Germany. It is Theo's task to search for a suitable place for them all in America. For someone who specializes in growing and maintaining subtropical plants, New York is not a good place. So Theodore Lowenstein gets on the next Greyhound bus and six days later he's in California.

When I meet Theodore Lowenstein again two years later, his name is Theo Löwenstein and he's a businessman. At least that's the information I get from the slightly faded manuscript of a radio essay by Süddeutscher Rundfunk from 1966. It deals with the "German Jewish Club of 1933," a "forgotten chapter of emigration," as its subtitle explains, and it looks as though it was Theo Löwenstein who founded this club for émigrés in Los Angeles.

And why not? There were reasons aplenty to start such a club: between 1930 and 1939, more than 2,500 German-speaking Jews had come to the greater LA area, and between then and 1945 another two thousand would follow.

And yet there's something that puzzles me: if the founder of the club was a businessman by the name of Löwenstein, that would have had to have been Theo's brother Joseph, but in 1933, the year the club was founded, Joseph hadn't yet arrived in the country.

This, however, is not a problem but rather a solution. Or at least a starting point. That is to say, after initially tracking the wrong man (Joseph), who supposedly had the right job (gardener), it seems that

XI

this time I met the right man (Theo), except that he supposedly has the wrong job (businessman).

But because things here are all muddled up—going wrong anyway, with nothing being quite as it seems—I decide to ignore the matter of the "businessman" and instead focus on the German Jewish Club of 1933, since that could be the missing link that will lead me from Theo Löwenstein, a resident of downtown LA, to the San Remo Drive property. In his diary entry of July 17, 1942, Thomas Mann mentions an "honorary membership certificate," and for all I know it was issued by the very club that Theo Löwenstein founded.

This club, however, doesn't have a formal structure until 1936, which is why Theo Löwenstein only becomes president that year. For two years, he's in charge of the club. When he retires, there are over eight hundred active members, and a newspaper with a circulation in the thousands.

The newspaper meets a very real need since the club's responsibilities have grown over time to include "cultural education for the new homeland" and "presentations of like-minded friends and Americans," as well as general advice and career guidance for new arrivals. The role of mediator is worthwhile—and effective. With the help of the club, every year up to two hundred émigrés find a job. The German Jewish Club remains a point of contact for many, especially since the establishment of a Cultural Section in 1937, which organizes regular lectures, concerts, theater performances, sports courses, and art seminars. The club's program even includes summer camps for children.

After 1940, when the club has become firmly established in LA's artistic and cultural scene, the "celebrity émigrés" finally make an appearance, but as America enters the war in late 1941, the focus shifts from culture to politics, and instead of selling concert tickets as before, the club now collects money for the purchase of a fighter plane that it intends to donate to the American military. Almost $50,000 is raised in this way.

And yet, in spite of all this information, I learn nothing of Theo Löwenstein's subsequent fate, and it's almost as if I've ended up in another cul-de-sac in my search for him. However, when I read the recollections of a man who was born as Wilhelm Ernst Stadthagen in Berlin in 1892, but who calls himself William Ernest Stagen after 1943 and under this name gives an interview in LA in 1972, I know that I am still on the right track.

Stagen, who was a successful real-estate entrepreneur at the time, was not only president of the club for many years, but also knew Thomas Mann, who wrote to him in 1950 and declared that he would be happy to give another lecture there. Yet this is just trivia. What really matters is the fact that Stagen knows things about the club that are not written down anywhere else. And so I learn that Theo Löwenstein was not only the founder and first president of the club, but also an accomplished gardener. In addition, Stagen recalls, Theo Löwenstein was an organizational talent who managed, over time, to transform a small and disparate group of émigrés into a genuine community whose members not only met regularly but also helped one another to find work. Stagen doesn't mention Thomas Mann in this context, but I can put two and two together. As this story is intent on fairness and balance, it is no wonder that the presidential gardener should come across the presidential writer as he is looking for work …

In financial terms, however, Theo Löwenstein is more in the lower middle class, but he is fortunate enough to no longer have to make ends meet on his own. His wife has joined him with their daughter and they now live together in the city, and his brother Joseph, called Joe, has arrived in LA as well. Theo had sent him some documents and advised him to present himself as a gardener when entering the country. The trick worked, and Joseph Löwenstein successfully obtained a visa and relocated from Nazi-controlled Germany to America. From 1934 on, Los Angeles is his home too.

In the meantime, Theo buys a piece of land near the small town of Vista, about a hundred miles south of Los Angeles, to grow avocados. He keeps his residence in LA but moves from downtown to the westside, first to Genesee Avenue and then to Gardner Street. He eventually buys a small house on Croft Avenue in 1940. In the census that year, Theo Löwenstein states that he is working sixty hours a week. One year later, on August 14, 1941, he stands next to Thomas Mann on the construction site on San Remo Drive and starts planning his garden.

At this point, however, there are not many lemon trees left on the property. Schlesinger and his people cut down most of them a few weeks ago to make room for the house, which was originally supposed to be 144 feet long by 43 feet wide. A modified building plan dated July 2 reduces its size to 102 by 32 to cut costs. But even the smaller house still takes up a lot of space, as a concrete driveway, motor court behind the house, paved entrance area, and two terraces all add to the building's footprint. The additional wing containing the study and the passageway linking it to the house are not even included in this calculation.

Thus, instead of trees, piles of building material rise toward the Californian sky, while the floor plan of the future house begins to emerge in the shape of ground beams and joists. Since the house must be anchored in the ground and should last for a while, the architect has instructed the builders to use only Wolmanized wood for all timberwork beneath the floor, because this does not rot away so easily. If all goes well, it can last for many decades thanks to being pressure treated with copper azole, a heavy-metal solution. This has a side effect: the timber is stained green from the treatment, and lying on the bare soil it creates an impression of the future lawn.

A short time later, on July 29, the wood frame has been erected and the villa towers over the building site in its full size — a wooden castle in the air.

It is time for Paul Huldschinsky to put his plans for the interior design of the house in motion, so he takes Katia to the city to pick out furniture. Thomas Mann steers clear of such ventures (and the tortures they entail for him).

By the time Thomas Mann returns to the property on August 11, the wood frame is already covered with plywood sheathing and plastered from the outside. And Schlesinger's people have started working on the interior. To his delight, Thomas Mann witnesses how one of the carpenters is fitting a little staircase into his little house, one that will lead directly from his study to his bedroom. "I attach great importance to always falling up the stairs," Thomas Mann had told a friend when he arrived in America. Three years later, this wish is about to be fulfilled. When the house is completed, Thomas Mann will fall upstairs. And he will even have a soft landing. In his very own bedroom. Onto his bed. Under his beloved silk duvet.

It is no wonder that three days later when Theo Löwenstein comes to talk about the garden, Thomas Mann insists on first taking him on a tour of the house. He guides him via his private staircase to the upper floor, leads him through all the rooms, and in the end proudly presents the large balcony that runs along the bedrooms and guest rooms spanning the entire south side of the house.

The view from up here is indeed extraordinary. To the west are the snow-capped Santa Monica Mountains and the huge ranch of entertainer Will Rogers, while Sunset Boulevard is to the east, less than two hundred yards from the house, hidden only by a row of palm trees. Yet it is to the south that the eye can travel the farthest, because on good days it is possible to see the entire California Riviera and the ocean all the way to the island of Santa Catalina, some thirty miles out to sea — the idyllic isle that will soon see the approach of a Japanese warship, ready to blow a few big holes into the Pacific Palisades of Los Angeles.

But we are not there yet, and for the time being the only Japanese in the area are those horticulturists who came into the country from the East at the beginning of the century and from whom Theo Löwenstein sources his flowers, plants, and ornamental shrubs. There is a good reason for that. Los Angeles, after all, has the greatest Japanese American population of any city in the entire United States. In 1941, almost twenty-five thousand of them live here, and of those who have professions, almost a third work in horticulture. If you need flowers, shrubs, or whole trees — or just want to mow your lawn — chances are you have to deal with one of them. When Theo Löwenstein — the Jew who studied landscape design in Berlin, worked as a flower grower in Italy, and planted orchards in Palestine — plans Thomas Mann's garden in Los Angeles in 1941, he can't possibly do without the American Japanese.

For five weeks, Theo Löwenstein plans, draws, and calculates. Then, on September 18, he presents his designs for the garden to Thomas Mann — and unlike the designs for the house, they are met with immediate approval. "It will certainly be the most beautiful property we have ever owned," Thomas Mann rejoices in his diary, and he also writes down the price. The whole venture is supposed to cost $1,100. Theo Löwenstein is hired.

Of course, he's not the only one. Paul Huldschinsky is also busy on behalf of Mr. Mann, except that his job is not the garden outside, but the rooms inside. To this end, Paul Huldschinsky makes regular trips to the city with Katia Mann to buy the furnishings that will turn the Californian villa into a home for the German poet, though not everything has to be bought new since some of their old furniture has finally found its way from Küsnacht through Princeton to California. The shopping sprees revolve primarily around furnishings for the bedrooms and guest rooms—although a table and chairs for the dining room, and a suitable sofa for the salon, must also be selected, along with new carpets and wallpaper, curtains, and garden furniture. As usual, Thomas Mann isn't concerned with hunting for household effects and he only participates in his wife's shopping trips with Paul Huldschinsky in spirit, if at all. He prefers the promenade in Santa Monica to the shopping streets of LA—and nightly notes each day's events in his diary in terms of debit (shopping) and credit (exercise).

08.22.1941: "K. downtown picking out curtain fabrics with 'Hulle.'" ("At noon short walk on my own in the sea breeze.")

09.10.1941: "K. downtown with Huldschinsky for furniture shopping." ("Had John drive me to Ocean Park and went for a walk.")

Only when it comes to his own room does Thomas Mann prefer to tag along.

09.24.1941: "At noon downtown with K. and Huldschinsky to select a wallpaper for my bedroom."

The ride downtown may have taken a bit longer on this occasion, because starting in mid-September a part of the road around San Remo Drive was torn open for resurfacing. This is an urgent task because the increasing number of houses in Pacific Palisades has also increased the number of cars. In early 1941, the local newspaper puts the number of villas under construction at sixty. And there are dozens more for which building permits have already been granted. No wonder the dirt-and-gravel mixtures on Capri, Monaco, and Romany Drives are being removed and the roads are getting a rock-hard asphalt surface.

At the beginning of October, on San Remo Drive, too, the planning of surfaces and ceilings begins. The architect Davidson has dropped by and brought samples of flooring for Thomas Mann's house, and while he's there, the ceiling design is discussed as well. If the colors are agreeable and the construction goes well, the house will supposedly be ready for move in by mid-December.

But things aren't going well. The wartime shortage of materials is now also becoming felt on the construction site. Workers are absent, and the delivery of the ordered windows and door frames takes several weeks. But there is another reason for the delays. Originally windows with steel frames were to be installed, but in the umpteenth revision of his building plan Davidson noted "Wood Windows and Doors instead of Steel!," and Schlesinger's documents also show wooden windows with the words "steel windows" overwritten with a large "Out!" And yet, for some unknown reason, in the end steel windows are delivered. As a result, both Davidson's building plans and Schlesinger's accounts will at some point be subject to a series of revisions, and no one can be sure whether the typewritten sums or those added in pencil behind them are the correct ones, not to mention the conundrum of an accounting item that has both a red tick and a question mark.

There are problems in the garden as well, but they are not as easily revisable, because the calculation behind them is much bigger than that of the architect Schlesinger. It is the Japanese attack on the

American naval base at Pearl Harbor and the subsequent reaction of the USA that cast a shadow on Thomas Mann's garden and threaten its existence. This is what happens …

A day after Japanese bombers sink a large part of the American Pacific fleet in Pearl Harbor on December 7, 1941, killing over two thousand men and finally dragging the USA into the maelstrom of international conflict, the United States declares war on Japan. But this is only the external reaction. The internal reaction targets the many American citizens of Japanese origin, who are henceforth regarded by the US government and local authorities as Japanese only, and thus as hostile foreigners. The fact that most of them have been living in America for decades, and many were even born here, is completely forgotten as emotions run high in the aftermath of Pearl Harbor. And this is why, just a few hours after the assault, the first "Japanese" are detained, and in the weeks and months that follow, the persecution continues.

Assaults, open discrimination, violence — the spiral of hatred and rage begins to spin ever faster and tear ever deeper into the country. And even though Japanese Americans are initially portrayed as loyal Americans in newspaper and radio reports — and regard themselves as such — this picture soon changes. Fear of the "Fifth Column" is rife, and further fueled by the American military and secret services. "We must worry about the Japanese all the time until he is wiped off the map," Lieutenant General John Lesesne DeWitt explains blatantly.

The sad climax of this development is finally marked by an executive order signed by President Roosevelt on February 19, 1942, ordering the deportation of all Japanese Americans from the West Coast to the interior of the country and their incarceration in camps there.

XII

Under the direction of DeWitt, Roosevelt's executive order is implemented immediately. Those affected often have only a few days to liquidate their businesses. Numerous plant nurseries and farms, in particular, are sold off for ridiculously low prices; others are abandoned, left to fall into disrepair, or ransacked. Where this does not happen, the enterprises of deportees are simply appropriated by "Americans" who henceforth treat them as their rightful possessions.

Those Japanese who are not arrested or deported to camps are forced to adapt their work to the war economy in service of the American state. The measure of their loyalty will henceforth be gauged in bushels harvested per acre to get the USA through its first year of the war.

At 1550 San Remo Drive, Ted Löwenstein is stuck. Until now he has bought his plants from Japanese growers in west LA, but now this is no longer possible. And that's not all. Many of the people who have been arrested and deported were more than mere business partners — they have become friends over the years. Now the Americans have turned them into enemies, driven them from their lands, gardens, and fields and taken them to remote areas in the interior, to camps in the middle of the desert.

German emigrants, too, are destined for such a fate, but they manage to dissuade the American government from implementing similar internment plans, not least thanks to the German Jewish Club founded by Theo Löwenstein. Together with others, the members of the club — which removed the word "German" from its name in October 1941 and since then has called itself only the "Jewish Club" — protest against the policy, hiring lawyers and mobilizing prominent advocates, including Thomas Mann. The latter has already written a letter to President Roosevelt on February 9, asserting that the German émigrés were opponents of totalitarianism and should not be treated as representatives of a hostile nation. This letter was followed up by a telegram drafted by the author Bruno Frank and signed by Thomas Mann, Albert Einstein, and other exiles. This telegram was also addressed to Roosevelt and resulted in both Thomas Mann and Bruno Frank — as well as the representative of the Jewish Club, Felix Guggenheim — speaking at the beginning of March in front of the Tolan Committee that is responsible for making recommendations for further action against the German émigrés.

And the protest is indeed successful. Although at the end of 1941 naturalization applications from German expatriates are suspended, the deportation plans for the spring of 1942 get taken off the table. There are some restrictions, but the measures against German "enemy aliens" are far less severe than those against the "Japanese." Instead of permanent detention in unfamiliar barracks, the German émigrés are placed under temporary curfews in their own apartments and houses. From now on it is mandatory to be at home between eight p.m. and six a.m., and during the day it isn't permitted to move more than five miles from one's home. It's hardly surprising that some émigrés should start to think of California as a kind of luminous prison, with sunbeams for bars.

Since many of the exiles live close to each other, however, the ban doesn't result in isolation, but rather in an increased number of visits to friends and acquaintances, which soon leads to a lively sense of community in Pacific Palisades, the emergence of various salons and societies, and an unprecedented number of private invitations (not to mention noninvitations).

Thomas Mann, on the other hand, can move freely. He has held Czech nationality since November 1936 and, like the rest of his family, is unaffected by the curfew.

But the passport issued by the Czech Republic, then sent to Switzerland and affirmed there by an oath of naturalization, is of no use to the German writer if his Jewish landscaper can no longer buy plants for a Californian property from Japanese gardeners in Los Angeles.

And yet, while Thomas Mann's garden isn't growing and construction of his house is proceeding at a sluggish pace by the end of 1941, gardens are being planted everywhere. All over LA, people are tinkering and digging on their properties …

"Dig for Victory" is the slogan adopted by the City of Los Angeles — and in Pacific Palisades, it's taken literally. In the spring of 1942, the local fire station digs up a large plot of land and lets people grow salad, potatoes, and cucumbers on it. Many others follow suit, and soon millions of Americans are tilling the soil, sowing, planting, and harvesting — with considerable success. Within a year, some 40 percent of all vegetables produced in America will come from front yards, side streets, and backyards.

Later on, Thomas Mann will also get his own vegetable patch, but now that Ted Löwenstein can't make any progress in the garden, most of Schlesinger's people have been drafted into the army, and the remaining workers are suffering from a lack of materials and motivation, the first thing to do is to furnish the interior of the house. In December 1941, the living and dining rooms are painted, then a suitable panel wood is selected for the library and hundreds of dollars' worth of fitted carpets and linoleum are purchased — the foundation for the Persian rugs that will arrive later.

In any case, Thomas Mann is satisfied with the progress made on the house and on January 5, 1942, he convenes a "color conference." Schlesinger and Davidson are invited, in addition to Huldschinsky, and the result can be summed up in a single word: at the end of the meeting, Thomas Mann notes "Außentönung," meaning "exterior tint," into his diary, and soon the house gleams in pristine white.

When I look at the result in a photo seventy-five years later, however, it seems as though someone had smeared the façade with black paint soon after it had been painted.

What may at first appear to be vandalism turns out to be a proliferation of ivy leaves growing out of the railing planters on the balcony, with a particularly thick strand of ivy sprawling across Thomas Mann's study.

When I look a third time, however, I realize that someone has tried their hand at a kind of photomontage and painted ivy leaves on the picture or retouched it in some other way.

I am reminded of Japanese ink drawings, but there are no Japanese people to be seen for miles, and the rationale for the montage remains obscure. Perhaps the person who painted the fictitious ivy leaves into the photo wanted to jump ahead in time and give an impression of what the house would look like one day. Or maybe they wanted to go backward in space, to the place Thomas Mann came from, and create an image of old Europe with an ivy-covered house.

But these are all just conjectures, fictions based on fictions, especially since I can't even say exactly when and by whom the ivy was added. There is no information about this in the archive.

But who knows, perhaps the tendrils and leaves do not imitate any real plants, but are only intimations of another fiction Thomas Mann will commit to paper between 1948 and 1950. In his novel *The Holy Sinner*, which takes place in late-medieval Rome, he will describe a

"balustrade overgrown with ivy whence one has a view of the hill of
the Foundation of our City and our most ancient shrines."

Here, on San Remo Drive — this fictional piece of Italy amid the
reality of California — the house itself lies on top of the hill and is
surrounded by lemon trees, avocados, and palm trees. The balcony
may not yet be overgrown, but the entire balustrade is already fitted
with planters, and it won't be long before the first blossoms appear
on the façade. But the back of the house hasn't been forgotten either.
A large pergola stretches from the garage to the entrance of the house,
and the first tendrils of a climber wind their way up its wooden
columns.

The family's domestic foundation has now, finally, been reestablished,
and Thomas and Katia Mann move into their new home on February 5, 1942.

Two days later, the kitchen range has broken, the heating system fails,
and servants of many years have quit. In the library there are not
enough books to fill the shelves and in the study there is "confusion
and disgruntlement" because the venetian blinds don't harmonize
with the curtains — and, to make matters worse, the Chinese bowl
that adorned Thomas Mann's desk for many years has been lost
during the move.

After leaving the house on Amalfi Drive, Thomas Mann installed
himself provisionally in the bedroom and thus moved from one temporary arrangement to the next. His mood is sour, lunch is served
late despite the table bell, and the new servants are "adverse people"
who should, in his opinion, "be removed soon."

The fact that they are from Germany and had to flee just like the
Mann family doesn't help the Hahn couple who've just taken up the

position. On the contrary. "Since we have the German couple, hardly a word of English is spoken in the house, as most tradesmen and suppliers also turn out to be German-speaking."

But there is another reason why one doesn't want to have such servants in the Mann household, why one complains of their "ignorant semi-education," why one wishes to "return to the friendly Negro tribe." This reason lies much deeper and will only be revealed later. For now, however, things take their course. On February 24, the Hahn couple is handed their notice of dismissal, effective March 15. Since they have no inclination to remain in the house for that long, however, they disappear the next morning.

So the house empties again, but even without the servant's room being occupied, Thomas Mann asks himself: "Why the huge living room (which is still a wasteland) and the many children's rooms?"

At least the matter with the wasteland is cleared up shortly afterward when Thomas Mann calls the contractor Schlesinger "to speed up the necessary carpentry work." The result: carpenters rush to the scene, straighten doors, assemble cabinets, and insert the still-missing drawers.

When the final work is completed at the beginning of March, Schlesinger presents the bill: $24,000 was estimated, and slightly over $26,000 is spent in the end. But this isn't so much due to general inflation or rising prices as to the owner's special wishes—an extra shower here, a special render there, a few extra paving jobs, a fence, a bit of fancy wiring … only $2,000 extra isn't all that much. And anyway, when building houses on the California Riviera it's always better to have slightly higher figures on the bill since there is an ordinance for new builds which states that—depending on the location—each home must cost, at minimum, between $12,500 and $25,000.

There are reasons for this regulation: after all, people want to remain among their peers, although this is of course not only a question of money but also of taste. Hence, before construction could begin the plan for the house had to be submitted to the local architectural committee, which not only considered the house's prospective appearance but also made sure that it was situated at a minimum distance from the street.

The garden in front made it easy to achieve the minimum distance, and Davidson's design did not cause any problems despite all the changes. It is a clean, unembellished house which—compared to the other houses in Pacific Palisades, and Davidson's other works—appears almost understated. While Davidson may not be one of those uncompromising artist-architects who construct hyper-modern living machines or put people into hard glass boxes, the "International Style" he subscribes to does espouse mainly linear, cubic forms. Davidson himself prefers houses with two wings whose angles to each other are obtuse—i. e., as open as possible. In the case of the villa on San Remo Drive, it is the corridor and the study behind it that form the second wing opposite the "main house." Davidson himself has, as always, measured everything very precisely and specified the desired opening in the plan at 108 degrees—in view of his highly detailed considerations, this number was probably deliberately chosen, since it matches the congruent interior angles in a regular pentagon.

But there is something else that distinguishes Davidson's houses from those of the architectural avant-garde of the time, since his primary objective is to build houses dominated by serenity, relaxation, and cheerfulness. The path toward the whole, he believes, should be charted in detail, like a plan that determines the future shape of a house on paper. Davidson does not like to alter his building plans. His calculations are too long and too precise, he thinks them over too carefully before finally putting them all together. In the case of the villa on San Remo Drive, however, he reached his limits with this approach. Numerous revised sketches and crossed-out drawings on the building plan bear witness to this. And yet, if Thomas Mann and his wife Katia had had their way, it would not have come to this. The two would have preferred to move into a traditional villa, with a balcony supported by large columns, stone balustrades, tall windows with mullions, and brown wood paneling in the salon, as well as a large hip roof adding a classic crown to the building—a house that served as a pastiche of itself and its inhabitants from the day they moved in, like the one they remember from Poschingerstrasse in Munich.

A house like this was out of the question for Davidson. And a large hip roof wasn't an option, as he prefers to build elegant flat roofs. On the California Riviera, however, flat roofs are prohibited, which meant that a compromise had to be found, and so they agreed on a slightly sloped construction, a so-called composition roof.

But Davidson hasn't left it at that. As always, he had a plan, and he's made sure the roof protrudes slightly from all sides of the house. This has two advantages: not only are the walls protected from rain, but the south-facing windows on the second floor are also protected from too much direct sunlight. This is all the more important because the profusion of glass on the south side was not really to Davidson's liking and given the Californian climate and the hillside location, he would have preferred to place the extensive window surfaces on the other sides of the house. But he had to comply with his client's wishes on this point, even though Thomas Mann will later regret his decision and repeatedly complain about the heat in his bedroom.

It is thanks to Davidson that the overheating of the rooms will rarely spread to the ground floor. He believes that architecture should

XIII

always encompass a protective function, and applied this idea to the planning of the lower floor as well, except that this time it was not the roof but the large balcony which he designed in such a way that it protruded well beyond the rooms below. Though the maid's room has disappeared completely into the shade and is only modestly supplied with light and air through its tiny windows, the dining and living rooms, both of which are extensively glazed on the south side, are mostly spared the problem of overheating. The cantilevered balcony also provides shelter from the heavy rain showers that will come up from the sea more frequently than the image of sunny California would have us believe, making the building "waterproof," as Davidson says.

Davidson himself was, of course, experienced enough to highlight these advantages at the planning stage. And so Thomas and Katia Mann let him have his way — at least on these points — and have concluded: "And so we now live in a modern house. We like it anyhow."

A big "anyhow" seems to be Ernst Schlesinger's constant companion too. Even though he did everything in his power to finish the villa within the agreed 140 days, the war and an increasing shortage of manpower and materials meant that the deadline couldn't be met, and in the end, almost 180 construction days were logged. But those weren't the only problems. The initial modifications made to the footprint and room layout also resulted in delays and additional work. Schlesinger was clever enough to talk down the authorities on the necessary conversion measures and to reduce the value of his work on paper to avoid having to submit completely new applications. And his prudence went further than that: he also made provisions for himself, drafting the contract with the Mann family in such a way that part of the payment was due before the completion of the house and he couldn't be held responsible for any delays caused by "force majeure."

And yet a fundamental question remains unanswered because I still don't know how Schlesinger met the Mann family in the first place, nor how he procured the contract to build the house. In Thomas Mann's diaries and letters, there is no indication that any family member knew Schlesinger before the building of the house. And even after that, he is mentioned only once, when Katia complains in a letter to Thomas Mann's secretary Konrad Kellen that no trellis for climbers could be attached to the house, because it was not possible to drive any nails into the walls, which caused "renewed resentment against the gentlemen Schlesinger and Davidson." The question of how the contractor Schlesinger and the Mann family came together, however, is still left open. The only possible connection could have been via the painter Eugen Spiro, for whom Schlesinger vouched in 1940. After all, the Mann family and especially Erika had tried to bring Spiro to America ("It must be possible to get an affidavit for Spiro").

The name Schlesinger, however, does not appear in the list of those who, in Erika Mann's opinion, could provide such a sworn declaration, and there is nothing in Thomas Mann's records either. Eugen Spiro had painted Thomas Mann in Leipzig in 1928 during Mann's speech on the centenary of the Reclam publishing house and put the painting on the cover of the corresponding book, and the two exchanged letters after they had both emigrated to America, but Ernst Schlesinger isn't mentioned once in their correspondence.

Nor does it seem that the connection could have been established via Davidson, since the name Schlesinger isn't mentioned anywhere in his papers either, so all that remains for me is conjecture.

When Ernst Schlesinger boarded the SS *Oregon* in Le Havre on July 25, 1936, according to the passenger list there was another German on board. His name was Wolfgang Blech, and the two seem to have stayed in touch. When Wolfgang Blech married in December 1939, Schlesinger was his best man. At the time, Blech himself was one of the leading lights of the German Jewish Club, the same association that Theo Löwenstein founded six years earlier and of which Thomas Mann was an honorary member. Perhaps the connection has run along the famous three degrees of separation.

I can't say whether Schlesinger himself was active in the club, but that isn't really relevant. The networks of the German emigrants in LA were so strong that even outside the club, it was basically just a matter of time before they met each other, or remet, since quite a few of the Californian exiles had already been friends before emigration, or had at least known each other before—be it in Munich, where Paul Huldschinsky met Thomas Mann, or in Berlin, which was, so to speak, the germinal cell of the Californian émigré circles. It is sufficient to score a few red lines across the tangle for illustration purposes ...

Before emigrating to America in 1936, Ernst Schlesinger liaised with a woman by the name of Lella Firle in Berlin for many years, who in turn was the sister of Eugen Spiro's wife, Elisabeth. After the end of this relationship, Lella Firle met the merchant's son Theodor Simon in Berlin in 1933. They were introduced to each other at a bridge evening by Wolfgang Blech, who emigrated to America together with Ernst Schlesinger in 1936. As if that wasn't enough, Lella Firle and Theodor Simon also came to America in 1933, and it was Eugen Spiro who took them by car to the train station on the day of their departure. The marriage between Lella Firle and Theodor Simon, however, broke down at the end of the thirties. Lella then married another man in LA who called himself Albrecht Joseph and who in 1943 worked for several months on San Remo Drive as Thomas Mann's private secretary after his previous secretary, Konrad Kellen, who had also come from Berlin and emigrated to California, was drafted into the US

Army. Kellen was actually called Katzenellenbogen (meaning "cat's elbow" in German), but this wasn't a name that would open many doors in America. Many immigrants adopted new names. Theodor Simon, for example, called himself "Theodore Hutton" in exile and met his best friend from his Berlin days in LA in 1939—none other than Paul Huldschinsky. Huldschinsky had just arrived in Pacific Palisades at that time, and while he may not have been looking for a new name, he was indeed looking for a new house. After finding one on Via Florence, he learned that his friend Theodor had just been dumped by his wife—and Huldschinsky allowed him to stay at his place. Theodor Simon subsequently worked as a factotum in Huldschinsky's villa, cooking for the exiled bohemians who loitered in the dining room, and also remained in contact with Ernst Schlesinger—that is, his ex-wife's ex-lover. And they didn't only cross paths in Huldschinsky's residence, but also in an LA laundry, which Theodor Simon ran for a while with Ernst Schlesinger's brother Paul's brother-in-law. It was, therefore, no coincidence but rather part of the natural order of the Weimar-Republic-under-palm-trees that Schlesinger would come to Eugen Spiro's aid and stand surety for him when he emigrated to America in 1941, since, as he wrote in his declaration of support, he had known him for fifteen years and was a close friend of his. Schlesinger, however, was not the only one whom Spiro knew from his Berlin days, for he also had connections to the Huldschinsky family, having trained Paul Huldschinsky's niece as a press illustrator in Berlin, long before she also arrived in America and was, in turn, picked up by car from the train station by Theodor Simon.

In other words, these people's entanglements were as diverse as they were confusing. They were spun like an invisible cocoon around the exile community and especially around Thomas Mann, this "emperor of all German émigrés." Ernst Schlesinger was part of this network, and when Thomas Mann looked around for a contractor, he didn't have to look for long …

What Ernst Schlesinger did after building Thomas Mann's house, however, remains a mystery. Not even his death left a trace — no obituary, no death notice, no papers, nothing. Ernst Schlesinger arrives from Germany, builds a house for Thomas Mann in California, and vanishes. The only thing I find on him is his entry in a Death Master File in the archives of the California Social Security Administration. According to this, Ernst Moritz Schlesinger lived to be only forty-seven years old and died in Los Angeles on July 4, 1949 — American Independence Day.

Ted Löwenstein, however, remains very much alive, and he is also very visible. After all, he has planted a multitude of shrubs and trees around the house — eucalyptus, cypresses, date palms, *Annona*, and bananas, as well as pepper trees and a *Caryota*, a palm species with twice-feathered leaves, also known as a fishtail palm, and finally, as a reminiscence of Thomas Mann's lost homeland, a *Thuja occidentalis*, an eastern arborvitae or "tree of life." But that's not all, because Ted Löwenstein has also planted a vegetable patch, a lawn, and flower bulbs. He's even planted a twenty-five-year-old olive tree in the ground and placed an American hydrangea at the entrance to the house. From where he sources all the seeds, seedlings, and plants remains his secret. There are also three birch trees on the property, very close to the entrance, at the back of the house — and even though Thomas Mann doesn't mention them anywhere and nobody else will say a word about them, there is a reason for their presence: the birch is Ted Löwenstein's favorite tree and the trio the trademark of his horticultural oeuvre, a signature in the form of a clump of trees, the arboreal autograph of a man who is proud of his work.

But there is something else because Ted Löwenstein is not only proud of his work, he is also — unbeknownst to anyone on the site, of course — colorblind. And so the black and white of the birch trees doesn't only bring a bit of variety to the green tones in the garden; to

Ted Löwenstein's eyes, it also provides necessary structure for the composition.

At any rate, Thomas Mann is delighted with the garden as a whole. When he begins to write a long letter to Hermann Hesse on March 15, he can draw on an embarrassment of riches — and quietly muster his descriptive powers to ensure that even Hesse, who lives in a villa in the Swiss canton of Ticino and is blessed with a view of Lake Lugano, will be green with envy as he reads.

"I work this way under external conditions for which I cannot be grateful enough — in the most beautiful study of all my life," Thomas Mann writes. "You should see the landscape around our house, with a view of the ocean; the garden with its palms, oil, pepper, lemon, and eucalyptus trees, the luscious flowers, the lawn that could already be mowed just a few days after planting. In such times, there is no shortage of cheerful sensations, and the sky here is cheerful almost the whole year round, emitting an incomparable light that beautifies everything."

The next day brings more cheerful weather, plus a fresh black domestic-service couple for errands, various letters, and a few framed pictures supplied by Paul Huldschinsky, which the latter duly puts up himself due to Thomas Mann's nonexistent ability to even drive a simple nail into the wall.

When Thomas Mann sees this, he is contented, returns to his study in buoyant spirits and continues to work on the letter by which he intends to impress Hermann Hesse with the beauty of his American home.

There is another letter which the diary does not mention on this sixteenth of March. Then again, the recipient is not a famous writer — he is basically nobody at all, neither someone well known nor anyone specific, because the other letter that Thomas Mann writes on this day, with the help of his secretary, is addressed "to whom it may concern." It states: "Mr. Ted Loewenstein is a landscaper with excellent botanical knowledge, great practical experience, and evident devotion to his work. He has transformed the uncultivated grounds surrounding my house into a tastefully arranged, thriving garden full of bloom."

It's a letter of recommendation Thomas Mann writes for Ted Löwenstein. And yet what sounds like a matter of course (a skillful and experienced gardener, a beautiful, blooming garden …) is only the prelude to a sentence the reasons for which, hidden deep under the writing hand, I failed to see when I first read it.

"I should like to add that although the agreement between us was made several months before the present difficulties in labor and supplies, he adhered strictly to the arranged price."

This small reference to the shortages in labor and materials remains silent about their reasons. And yet I would not have been able to write the story of Ted Löwenstein and the garden he created for Thomas Mann without this hint. It was this sentence that first pointed me toward a trail that leads far beyond the garden and the property, a trail that begins with the arrival of Japanese gardeners in the coastal towns and cities of California and ends with their deportation inland. That is to say, it *almost* ends there, because not only has Ted Löwenstein managed to successfully complete the garden for Thomas Mann despite all the difficulties, but the Japanese will also return, they will find their way out of the camps and move into the house of Thomas Mann …

But the story hasn't progressed that far yet — and Thomas Mann has to finish the letter to Hermann Hesse first, anyway. On March 17 it is finally done, and Thomas Mann notes the completion of the letter in his diary. But there's one more thing he does, even if the reader of the diary doesn't find out about it. Shortly before he ascends his private stairs to his bedroom on the evening of March 17, Thomas Mann takes a copy of his own *Magic Mountain* from the shelf, opens it, and writes a dedication on the endpaper: "To the landscaper Ted Loewenstein. ('He made the wasteland my magic garden'). Grateful for his work."

Ted Löwenstein will never see Thomas Mann again. He will continue to run his small nursery for a few more years, then give it up and try his luck at another profession. When he passes away in 1985, Thomas Mann's letter of recommendation will still be hanging on the wall of his study.

XIV

In the Exile of Exile, Old German Masters Feel at Home

This much is clear: Thomas Mann appreciates it when things take their usual course.

Getting up, washing, getting dressed, having breakfast, writing, going for a walk, having lunch, resting, drinking tea, dictating letters, eating dinner, listening to music, reading, sleeping—and then the whole thing all over again.

Getting up, washing, getting dressed, having breakfast, writing, going for a walk, having lunch, resting, drinking tea, dictating letters, eating dinner, listening to music, reading, sleeping.

Getting up, washing, getting dressed, having breakfast, writing, going for a walk, having lunch, resting, drinking tea, dictating letters, eating dinner, listening to music, reading, sleeping.

That's how it works.
Only it won't work out for long.

When Thomas Mann takes his wife Katia for a walk around Pacific Palisades on the afternoon of March 22, 1942, he meets an Englishman who lives a little above them. His house, like so many here, has just been finished, but the fellow has already torn out all the shrubs and trees in his freshly planted garden, and he has even had the lemon trees and palm trees that had long stood here cut down. Asked about the reasons for his actions, he claims to be afraid of Japanese bombs.

And that fear is entirely justified. It's been less than four months since the attack on Pearl Harbor, and the American defense lines are so weak that should the Japanese decide to attack the US directly, their

Kamikaze pilots would have no trouble finding targets. On the entire West Coast, a grand total of just three thousand American soldiers are deployed in the spring of 1942, with no more than fifty fighter planes and eighty-five bombers at their disposal. It is no wonder that some people in Pacific Palisades simply want to leave and sell their homes for laughable sums of money, while others are starting to set up citizen guards and patrolling the villas with guns slung over their shoulders, walking from hill to hill searching for people who look like their former gardeners, only this time are feared of wanting to dig up the land from the air.

And, of course, the inevitable happens, as it always does in such cases. If you look long enough, you see what you want to see … After a lone Japanese submarine attacks the Ellwood Oil Field on February 23, 1942, Japanese planes are spotted over LA during the night of February 24–25, whereupon air-raid sirens start howling around the city at 2:21 a.m., all lights go out, and the sky reveals its secrets in the darkness of night. A colonel counts twenty-five Japanese fighter planes as other "candy-shaped objects" are discovered in the sky, and a citizen armed with binoculars sees an armada of enemy hot-air balloons approaching from the sea, all carrying flares, prompting the commander of the 37th Coastal Artillery Brigade to shout "Fire!" before the sky above LA begins to explode.

When the dead are counted the next morning, there is only one. It's an American. He has suffered a heart attack as a result of stress caused by the shooting. But others have been affected as well. Numerous motorists have crashed into other vehicles in the sudden blackout, and several houses have suffered damage from shrapnel. There are no Japanese to be found, however, and it doesn't take long before the whole thing turns out to be a false alarm, which means the Americans weren't shooting at the enemy but rather at a weather balloon and, after that, at their own antiaircraft shells exploding in the sky.

Thomas Mann doesn't say a word about these events in his diary and prefers to recount how he showed his friend Bruno Walter and his family the new house, for which they expressed their highest admiration. There is no mention of any nocturnal skirmish, and even when he walks along San Remo Drive with his wife a few days later and sees trees felled on other properties, this is obviously no reason for Thomas Mann to become anxious. "Beautiful walk," he notes in his diary, and only when he reads in the newspapers on April 4 that an air raid on Lübeck has destroyed the "Buddenbrook House" does he begin to think about his own house, all the more so since his daughter Erika has come to the conclusion that their property would "burn unusually well under hostile circumstances."

But what to do? Dig up the trees in the garden to protect the house? Not a good idea, because Thomas Mann loves his garden. Besides, what would he tell Hermann Hesse? That he cleared everything because the ocean view wasn't good enough and he wanted to be able to see all the way to Japan?

Then again, how about going down to the fire station and joining the fire department's safety course for the residents of Pacific Palisades? According to the newspaper, three thousand of them have already taken part and learned how to extinguish bombs and how to cut firebreaks into the underbrush. Thomas Mann, though, can't even hammer a nail, which is why this option also falls as flat as the trees on the neighboring properties.

There is always the option of registering with the Pacific Palisades Defense Council, putting a steel helmet on his head and driving around in the firetruck that its members have just purchased. Sadly, Thomas Mann doesn't have a driver's license — and steel helmets are not his thing after all the bad news that reaches him from his old homeland.

And so Thomas Mann does what he does best: he dispatches his wife to a first-aid course, deploys his daughter Erika to a meeting to discuss the fire hazard from bombs, and otherwise relies on the two 155-caliber field guns the Army has stationed in Pacific Palisades to secure the coast and land.

All this done, Thomas Mann carries on as before.

Getting up, washing, getting dressed, having breakfast, writing, going for a walk, having lunch, resting, drinking tea, dictating letters, eating dinner, listening to music, reading, sleeping.

Getting up, washing, getting dressed, having breakfast, writing, going for a walk, having lunch, resting, drinking tea, dictating letters, eating dinner, listening to music, reading, sleeping …

… and the only thing that upsets him is the fact that a local resident who stops by to inform him about the imminent threat of fire enters the house "through the wrong door."
In other words, the man has traipsed through the garden instead of walking up the driveway, but the lawn has survived the visit intact—and the Japanese also desist from bombing Thomas Mann's flowers.

Instead, it is the neighbors who cause trouble. Thomas Mann certainly dislikes most of them. He is particularly suspicious of Americans from the film industry. And when his routine is disturbed by them, his good mood goes … "After tea a cocktail visit in the neighborhood, Thomas, Mr. and Mrs., he very stupid and unpleasant; another couple. A waste of time."

Perhaps he would think differently about the "movie riffraff" and their supposed stupidity if he knew what the wife of actor Joseph

Cotten, who played the lead role in Orson Welles's *Citizen Kane* and also appeared in Paul Huldschinsky's film *Gaslight*, tells a newspaper reporter one day. Asked if she greets Thomas Mann on his daily walk, she says: "Oh no, I've never met him. He always looks so forlorn that whenever I see him coming I rush into the house and start playing Beethoven till he walks by. I think that cheers him up."

Well, it isn't known whether this serenade really cheers up Thomas Mann, but there is something that verifiably gives him pleasure in 1942 — and that is his desk. In February, this faithful piece of furniture has just moved into the new house. It arrived from Princeton the month before, but Thomas Mann couldn't use his beloved desk immediately. The years of exile had left their mark. A cabinet maker was called in, the mahogany was polished, and everything was gleaming again.

When the table was ready, it looked as if Thomas Mann had just bought it from the Munich antiques dealer Bernheimer. That was in 1928. Or 1929. Nobody knows exactly. But it doesn't matter, anyway. There may be war outside, Japan may threaten California with fire, and the whole world may bomb itself back into barbarism — but in here, in Thomas Mann's study, the Old World has come into its own again and the New World is shut out behind the windows, no matter how much Thomas Mann is occupied with the news of the day or how many letters and political speeches he writes. "When I sit at my desk in the morning and immerse myself in the minds and hearts of the characters I want to bring to life, sometimes I really don't know where I am — in Munich? Küsnacht? Anyway, I'm obviously at home, and that's the main thing."

And indeed it is: the desk is Thomas Mann's home — a small, constant sanctuary in changing times, a time capsule that travels with him from place to place. Here everything is assigned a spot, is sorted, set, and solid … a servant figurine from an Egyptian tomb, a photo of his wife when she was young, a portrait of Savonarola, a little silver plaque featuring the old Tolstoy, the ram-headed Egyptian deity Khnum, a plaster statue of a king, a jade jar, stones, a fossilized sea lily, an elephant tusk, a Japanese vase, a bowl from China, a cigarette box from Russia, writing paper from Switzerland, a calendar, a notepad, and a bronze Buddha, all framed by two brass candlesticks, imitations from Schiller's desk in Jena …

Thomas Mann sits amid all of this and writes, and only occasionally a servant comes in, dusts everything off, and is asked not to mess anything up.

When no servant is available, the family members who are present must help out, and so it happens that Thomas Mann's nephew has the task of bringing him a morning drink at 11:15 a. m. every morning. An egg yolk and two teaspoons of sugar, all whisked and completed with Cinzano — this is served to him.

"I came down the corridor and didn't knock, I shouldn't knock, I just opened the door and put the drink on his desk. And he would sit there, not even pretending that someone was in the room, and then I would march out again."

It is this space, removed from the vicissitudes of time, and the constant repetition of an immutable routine that give Thomas Mann the peace of mind he needs to work. But there is a new American addition, too: since it was moved into the new house, the old desk sports an electric clock. Thomas Mann's patron Agnes Meyer gave it to him as a present, and when Thomas Mann enters his study in the morning, he always marvels at how it manages to count the days. "How does the creature know that it must change both digits from the 29th to the 30th, but only the second digit from the 30th to the 31st, and that the first digit must disappear from the 31st to the 1st?"

He doesn't have an answer to that question. But maybe there isn't one, maybe in a room where—when the venetian blinds are closed—you don't know whether you're in Munich, Zurich, or Pacific Palisades, and where you can't tell whether it's 1930, '36, or '42, any kind of chronometer is an impossible proposition anyway and the changing date is only there to remind you of an outside world where things do in fact change.

And change they do. On February 14, 1942, the day Thomas Mann sits for the first time at his old desk in his new house, the British Air Ministry instructs the Air Officer Commanding-in-Chief RAF Bomber Command to begin saturation bombing cities in the German Reich.

Thomas Mann's house is being saturated, too, but instead of destruction, there is the restoration of everything that had been salvaged from Germany, with the gaps left by paintings, furniture, and other things expertly filled by Paul Huldschinsky. And so, after the desk in the study has been restored, the shelves put up, and all the books put in place, the rest of the house will be completed after March 1942. In the dining room, the family silver is displayed on the sideboard for symbolic purposes, while the Empire wardrobe is set up in the living room. A carpet from Küsnacht is spread at the Manns' feet, and the candles in the candelabra that belonged to their grandparents in Lübeck also begin to glow. Mirrors set the scene—the world returns to its former glory.

In other ways, too, final touches are being made. The gramophone arrives—"the good old Victrola"—and the reading chair from Munich, with its retractable footrest, will follow soon. And thus, in the course of the year 1942, everything falls into place piece by piece: the furniture and the awnings, the carpets and the wallpapers, the pictures and the bookshelves. It's as if a museum is being built: *The Old*

Homeland, a permanent exhibition within four walls. And only occasionally is there a change of exhibition …

"Visit from Huldschinsky, who brought the framed reproductions. Hanging and re-hanging pictures. Goethe corner in the study with the portrait of Lotte. Renoir and the old German master in the living room."

The exterior of the house on San Remo Drive may be kept in a modern style, but the interior is basically one big replica, a replica of a lost world, a German enclave in California, a repossession of the American Dream.

The one who's helped Thomas Mann to realize this dream is Paul Huldschinsky. It was not an easy task, however, as Thomas Mann's wife Katia was in charge of furnishing the house, as she's in charge of all practical things in life — and Paul Huldschinsky soon had a problem despite his proven good taste.

"I don't know what to do with the old furniture from Lübeck," he confided in his friend Theodor Simon. "It's not really that hard, but Katia always says no."

The "no" did not refer to the furniture itself, however, but to its arrangement and placement, especially as the items they had brought along from Europe were not enough to fill the house. New acquisitions were therefore unavoidable and the question of how Lübeck and Los Angeles could become one remained open for a long time.

When Paul Huldschinsky finally presented furniture in the American colonial style, placed it next to the furniture of their German grandparents, and thus created the pastiche inside the house that had remained elusive on the outside, Katia was satisfied and gave him a yes.

And indeed, the "early American furniture" does not stand out among the old pieces; it blends in and becomes a part of that upper-middle-class world that consists of dark cabinets, sturdy armchairs, and layered rugs on oak flooring. Add to that the family silver on the sideboard, the white porcelain on the table, and the old German masters on the wall, and you have created an old, new home. These are rooms as the Mann family knew them from Munich and Küsnacht—though Paul Huldschinsky has also incorporated his own experiences from Berlin. It's probably no big surprise that the bookshelves in Thomas Mann's Californian study look exactly like those Paul Huldschinsky had fitted in Berlin's Tiergartenstrasse in 1927—the villa now used by National Socialist euthanasia officials to plan, with the help of cover organizations, the "beautiful deaths" of those they regard as worthless.

Thomas Mann, however, is aware of this and is keen for his former compatriots to hear about it too: "In German hospitals and clinics, the severely wounded are brought to their deaths with poison gas, along with the elderly, the infirm, and the mentally ill," he writes at the end of November 1941. He then records this speech in the NBC studio, has it pressed onto a record and sent by airmail to New York, where it is cabled to the BBC in England to be finally broadcast on a long-wave signal to the German Reich. It is one of the last public-awareness campaigns against the mass murder of disabled and sick people. By 1942, the subject of euthanasia largely disappears from British propaganda programs.

Meanwhile, in California, the work in the house is nearing completion, and on April 6, 1942, it is finally finished. The last craftsmen are gone, the still-missing curtains are hung, and all the books are placed on the shelves, well organized and sorted.

Thomas Mann is happy. It's not the first house he's owned, but it's the most beautiful of all. Two days later, he writes a thank-you letter to the architect Davidson, saying that he has "combined the practical and tasteful with true virtuosity in the construction and layout of your building." And the building even has a positive effect on Thomas Mann's fraught state of mind: "In times of so deeply depressing circumstances a harmonious home environment is of great spiritual significance."

Well, whatever Davidson replied to that—to him the house doesn't seem to have been all that wonderful. When twenty-five years later he draws up a list of the houses he has designed, Thomas Mann's villa won't feature on it, and Davidson won't mention the house on San Remo Drive anywhere else either. As far as we know, he doesn't present it to potential customers even once, and others seem to take a similar view.

When the architectural photographer Julius Shulman, who documented many of the houses built by Davidson, is asked in 1976 which of the architect's buildings he considers being of special significance, the villa on San Remo Drive won't come up. It won't even make it onto the list of houses of lesser importance, and in the extensive correspondence between Davidson and the architectural historian Esther McCoy that spans many years, the Thomas Mann House will only make a marginal appearance. The magazine *California Arts & Architecture* is the only publication to mention the villa: in its December 1942 issue, it runs a short article highlighting the "close collaboration" between owner and architect, and also quoting from Thomas Mann's letter to Davidson.

Davidson himself does not seem to have attached much importance to this citation, not least because some of his previous houses had been placed much more prominently in the magazine, and it almost seems as if he regards the villa as a foreign body, if not in its outer then in its inner landscape, a piece of "nostalgic Germany" amidst the California hills. In his notebook, he calls the house "a compromise," yet adds, "I'm not ashamed of it."

Nor is there any reason to be ashamed. But the tight budget, the multiple changes to the plan, the special wishes of the Mann family, and the restrictions in the Riviera area ensured that while the house remained true to type in a way, it only partially reflected Davidson's architectural style.

And yet the outer form of the Villa seems to have caused Davidson the least headaches. What is much worse for him is the interior design of the rooms, which he dislikes so much that he'll never have any photographs taken of them and will be happy throughout his life that very few images ever show what the house looks like inside, because what he sees there is too German, too nostalgic, too Old World for his liking. The ivy that someone painted on the picture of the newly completed house will over the years grow inward in Davidson's eyes.

It's as if the New World has once again sought equal esteem.
There is Julius Ralph Davidson, who had worked as an interior designer in Berlin before emigrating, but who later avoided any advertising with the Thomas Mann House and didn't need it either. He had been in the country since 1923 and had already built a large number of houses, even though he was reserved, even shy, and received all of his commissions through letters of recommendation from clients and friends, and even rejected some jobs when the clients proved to be unfriendly, selfish, or simply too chatty. After the construction of the Thomas Mann House, he will participate in the Case Study House Program, a large-scale attempt to combine new and experimental forms of residential construction with social and economic considerations. The program runs from 1945 to 1966 and its initiators are concerned with nothing less than the future of American construction. Davidson will design three model homes, which

will be built between 1946 and 1948. They should be airy, light filled and modern, built from industrially manufactured materials.

Paul Huldschinsky, on the other hand, is a very different man. He had initially worked in Berlin as an interior designer, but after emigrating to America he hoped to gain attention through his work on the Thomas Mann House — and also needed it, because he had received hardly any commissions since his arrival in 1938, even though he was anything but reserved and threw parties that were so exhilarating that even seasoned bon viveurs still talked about them years later.

Following the interior design of the Thomas Mann House, Paul Huld-schinsky will create period sets for the film studios of Hollywood. When *Gaslight* is shot in 1943, he will design part of its late-Victorian décor. The film will be released in 1944 and will receive seven Oscar nominations, and two awards, the following year. One of these will go to Paul Huldschinsky for "Interior Decoration." When asked how he came up with his ideas, he'll say he had furnished the rooms just like his own back in the day when he was living in Berlin. And even if this is only half the truth and the film's design is also based on drawings and photographs from the late-nineteenth century, it will be a convincing story. In any case, there is not even a hint of any forward planning here. And Paul Huldschinsky, who lacks the "factory and type fantasy" of which the modernists of his time could not get enough, will continue to work on reconstructions of the past and design sets for period dramas until his death. But *Gaslight* remains his most important work. There is a gloomy, oppressive atmosphere that emanates from the old-fashioned furniture, heavy plush curtains, and fireplace with a wrought-iron poker set …

And Thomas Mann? He enjoys his house, his study, and his garden, even though his son Golo and his wife Katia are fighting a desperate and "invigorating battle with the weeds."

Before vigor gives way to staleness and the weeds finally gain the upper hand, the garden must, of course, be shown off, and the new house also cries out to be presented. So Thomas Mann will invite friends and acquaintances to take the grand tour, have entire photo shoots taken of the property, and tell the rest of the world about the beauty of his Californian home in diary entries and letters.

06.14.1942: "We enjoy our house and garden every day."
07.12.1942: "Sitting on my bench in the garden with magazines."
07.15.1942: "Read magazines in the living room. Nice time."
Finally, on 07.31.1942: "We have a big domestic staff shortage."

It is the eternal dilemma — the employees in the Manns' California household turn over at a pace that's difficult to keep track of, even in retrospect. As soon as they're in the house, they're out again.

When the Mann family still lived in Princeton, things were different: there was continuity with regards to the servants and things, in general, were well organized. The family sat together in the living room, where Thomas Mann read from the newspaper and a black butler in a white jacket offered crackers.

Of course, the butler's name was John, and even though he looked very different from "our Marie in Munich," he did his job very well. "He even assembled the grandmother's candelabra."

And while John served crackers with one hand and conjured up the past with the other, his wife Lucy was busy in the kitchen, under Katia's supervision. And lo and behold, "The food tastes almost as good as at home."

Yes, in Princeton the Munich microcosm was still intact, and if the servants didn't know what to do or were unsure of their duties, Katia

Mann would jump in: "Mother will show the moon angels how to make dumplings, and she will make sure that they don't mess up anything on the desk. That would be all."

And it was indeed all. At least in Princeton. But in LA, things get more complicated. Lucy Long and her husband John had come with them to California in April 1941, but they left the Mann family in February 1942, a few days before moving into the new house. The reason was simple: John was ill, even though Thomas Mann saw things from a somewhat different perspective: "He had been feeble and not much use for a while," he noted in his diary. And then: "This is a real calamity for my wife, who has to hurry and look for new people for the first time in this country."

It shouldn't be the last time. In their ten years at San Remo Drive, the Mann family will change their domestic staff almost fifty times.

Anyway, when Lucy and John are gone, it doesn't take long for a new domestic-service couple to be hired, but after only a few days they're dismissed again. The Manns then try to convince Lucy to come back, but this fails and leads to the wife of a publisher friend helping out in the house, at least until an immigrant from Vienna is hired as a cook at the end of February, but she doesn't stay long either and disappears again in March. On August 4 a new girl finally arrives, but she leaves the house only three days later, to be replaced on August 16 by "a Negro couple from Texas." Ruth and Will stay for two months, and then he is drafted into the military and the wife of the publisher friend has to return once more until the "Negro girl Gussy" is brought into the house on January 2, 1943. Thomas Mann is quite satisfied with the culinary arts of "the maid" ("homemade lunch from pigeon and chocolate ice cream, very good"), and his wife Katia also considers "the darkie" to be "a very clever and reasonably industrious thing," since she provides her with relief in a household that suffers not only under the problematic wartime supply situation and its own, upper-middle-class entitlements, but also hosts numerous family members, friends, acquaintances, and other visitors, who, in turn, bring their own demands, wishes, and expectations with them.

In any case, it is not long before the girl Gussy turns up only sporadically and after June 30 she stays away for good, which is why the servants of acquaintances, the maids of neighbors, or the Manns' own children have to be conscripted for kitchen, household, and table service, acting as "mother's auxiliaries" for several months, until at the end of the year the diary finally records the "Arrival of an intelligent Negro woman as maid."

Her name is Myrtle, and she is always so tired after work that she puts on her nightgown, goes to bed in the maid's room, and starts snoring. So Katia Mann brings an additional helper into the house on August 16, 1944, but her stay is hardly longer than the entry she gets in Thomas Mann's diary: "New girl, old, white, who wanted to impose herself, kept over lunch and dismissed again."

A few months later, on January 7, 1945, when it is finally Myrtle's turn to leave, I pause in my reading, asking myself who this person really was, and — since no one else has done this before and I no longer feel like cataloging the stupendous chronology of entrances and exits — I start looking for her. It takes me a while to find her full name.

Myrtle Chatman, like so many others, hardly left a trace, even though, as I learn later, she worked in numerous villas in the hills west of LA and her husband Carl was a sought-after bartender in the salons of the rich and famous. But they had another life, and while Myrtle was working for Thomas Mann they were actively involved in the local church. It's an old bulletin of the Victory Baptist Church in LA that first puts me on their track—and I only notice the relevance of this track when I take a closer look at it the brochure. Myrtle Chatman is mentioned as president of the Women's Group, and it is always a good thing when a story not only features a presidential writer and a presidential gardener, but also a presidential domestic servant in a nightgown.

But there's more, because even though Myrtle Chatman will leave San Remo Drive in early 1945, she'll remember her work there for many years to come. When Thomas Mann dies in 1955, she will send his wife Katia a condolence card: "I read about Doctor Mann. This is from Myrtle Chatman. I worked for you two years. Remember? Love to all."
The picture on the card shows two candles and a bouquet, with a handwritten note: "I do hope you will receive this."

And the card does indeed arrive, just as a new girl arrives at San Remo Drive ten years earlier because, after Myrtle's departure, a replacement has to be found. So the National Association for the Advancement of Colored People's employment agency is called and a new domestic servant is ordered, and on February 5, Thomas Mann announces the "entrance of a new Negro maid."

Her name is Leona, but her cooking skills seem a little special because the diary reports "soup, brain and fruit jelly," which is why, when Leona is ill, Thomas Mann considers himself fortunate to be able to have "meals without the girl." In the long run, however, such a meal without help is not for him, and his wife Katia also can't do without help in the household. So a girl named Myra is hired, but in the eyes of the master of the house she proves to be "foolish" and soon has to make way for a new helper, who is in turn replaced after only four weeks on June 16, 1945, by a new "Negro maid," who, of course, will only stay for two months.

XVI

Katia Mann is "upset by the departure of the new, relatively useful Negro girl," prompting Thomas to announce five days later, on August 15, that a new "Negro Couple" has arrived that "seems useful and willing." Shortly thereafter, however, this couple also leaves, and all that remains and can be reused is an adjective from the earlier diary entry.

September 15, 1945: "New girl, white, seems useful."

But it seems the new girl doesn't hang around long either, because on October 4 the diary reports: "Entrance of a Japanese domestic service couple." And then: "These kind people, Vattaru and Koto by name, had lost their property in the cruel war of their own, they had become acquainted with the anguish of humiliation in the camp and sought to restore themselves economically by offering service."

That's enough. And it must be enough because I don't have any more information. Two names—Vattaru and Koto—and one shared fate, the internment camp.

The only question is: Where exactly were Vattaru and Koto interned? After Pearl Harbor, the Americans would eventually build close to a dozen "relocation centers" and hold more than 110,000 Japanese Americans captive in them.

As I rummage around a bit, I learn that those who lived in Los Angeles were almost all held in Manzanar Camp …

On the Joy of Misspellings

When it's established in March of 1942, the Manzanar internment camp in the Sierra Nevada represents the greatest possible contrast to Thomas Mann's property on San Remo Drive. Instead of a villa with domestic staff, there are barracks with military police. A barbed-wire fence stands in for the hedge, eight watchtowers replace the seven palm trees and the lemon tree, piles of construction rubble take the place of flower beds, and whereas a lush green lawn sprouts from the ground at the former, at the latter there is only dirt — covered with a fine layer of desert sand, for only the wind can move freely here in Manzanar.

A trip by car from Manzanar via Sunset Boulevard to LA isn't possible, and the view to the southwest — toward home, freedom, the Pacific — is blocked by 14,379-foot-high Mount Williamson, without access roads or mountain shelters, and so it isn't surprising that the internees, who let their thoughts wander away from their straw-filled gunny sacks and barren rooms out of the camp, don't end up in Los Angeles, some 240 miles away, but rather in a small, withered village to the north of the camp, which is appropriately named Independence. And that's already the better choice because those who let their dreams lead them southward end up in a forsaken whistle-stop named Lone Pine that only has one historical claim to fame: having lost 80 percent of its homes and 10 percent of its population to an earthquake.

It is here, then, beyond the beyond, that they live, the Japanese citizens of Los Angeles, and out of the eleven thousand internees that have been brought to Manzanar since March 1942, I now have to find those two who will begin their service in Thomas Mann's house in October 1945.

I am relieved when I discover a file in the digital repository of the

National Archives and Records Administration which lists all the Japanese housed in Manzanar. It reads like a telephone directory of Tokyo. However, typing in "Vattaru" does not bring up a single match.

That is, of course, no reason to give up. Perhaps, I think, Thomas Mann simply misspelled the name "Vattaru," since he misspelled things all the time. He never learned to spell his neighbor Lester Ziffren's name correctly for as long as he lived on San Remo Drive and kept scribbling strange dedications into the books he gave Ziffren ("To Lester Zifferer from his good nabour Thomas Mann").

If you habitually produce this kind of alphabet soup, you're bound to make a mess of the name of your Japanese gardener. So I try my luck … Wattaru, Vataru, Wataru … And bingo!

But there are eighty-two matches. The phonebook file presents me with a veritable village of Watarus. I have no way of telling which is the right one because the file contains no further information, and so I have no choice but to try my luck again with the name Koto and hope that it will be less common.

Fat chance! There are indeed only fifty-one Kotos on the list—but also plenty of women named Kotono, Kotome, Kotone, Kotoyo, Kotoe, Kotoji, Kotoko, and Kotora—and again it is quite possible that Thomas Mann didn't use his Japanese housekeeper's correct name in his diary entries.

In this way the list of potential candidates has grown to ninety-three, which makes a grand total of 175 people, combined with the Watarus, and I can only hope that two of these will belong together.

In principle, it's quite simple. I just have to cross-reference all Watarus and Kotos to see if any two of them have the same family name.

When I finish, I find not two but twenty people. Standing before me are:

Wataru and Koto Fujii
Wataru and Koto Kimura
Wataru and Kotome Kobayashi
Wataru and Koto Nakamura
Wataru and Kotoe Okamoto
Wataru and Koto Shimidzu
Wataru and Koto Tanaka
Wataru and Koto Watanabe
Wataru and Kotoye Watsuda
Wataru and Kotoyo Yamamoto

For a moment I imagine that all these Watarus and Kotos were in Thomas Mann's employ consecutively, that they went in and out of his house in turns, that some were dismissed, others rehired, an infinite string of Japanese domestic-service couples who provided continuity, if not in the household, then at least in the diary ... "kind people, Vattaru and Koto by name."

A story with twenty more-or-less identical housekeepers must inevitably end in a comedy of errors, but this treadmill of substitutions and replacements in Thomas Mann's household offers only limited amusement, and so I scour the internment files for further clues and strike off my list all those Watarus and Kotos who are too young, too old, too unmarried, or too anything else. When I am done, I am left with Wataru and Koto Shimidzu.

When Wataru and Koto Shimidzu are transported to Manzanar by bus on June 1, 1942, to be locked up there, the place is doubly alien to them because neither is used to either life in the camp or life in the desert.

Wataru is actually a sailor. He comes from a small town on the eastern seaboard of the main island Honshu and landed in America in 1919—aboard the SS *Tenyo Maru*, a passenger liner with its own floating opium den. The first few years after his arrival, Wataru takes every job he can get his hands on, then he finds work on a ship, the *Africa Maru*, a 475-foot colossus of steel that ferries passengers and payloads from one side of the Pacific to the other. Wataru's task is to shovel enough coal into the boilers for the ship to steam back and forth between Hong Kong, Yokohama, and San Francisco. Sometimes he also has to rake out the ashes or to retrieve new coal from the ship's bunkers—a dirty and dangerous job that leaves a scar on his face after just a few days. In June 1929, he finally has enough of this drudgery. When the *Africa Maru* sets sail in San Francisco, Wataru Shimidzu is not on board, but on a list of "deserting seamen."

Koto, on the other hand, tries to build up a life in America as a seamstress. Hailing from the south of the island Honshu, she came to the country in 1924, five years after Wataru. She has a small scar over her right eye and when she meets Wataru she notices that he has one too. Together they move into a small apartment at 1115 San Julian Street, a short distance south of downtown LA.

Here they live a simple life, which moves with the rhythm of their work. Koto makes garments and helps Wataru, who runs a wholesale store for fruit and vegetables. They have no children and never will, and the date of their marriage, November 21, 1933, is just a day like any other. The next morning, as usual, Wataru rises at half-past three, takes a new delivery of fruit and vegetables, sorts the goods, distributes them in boxes, and determines prices for the coming day. When this is done an hour and a half later, Wataru's store opens at five o'clock, and he, Wataru Shimidzu, only closes it again late in the evening.

That's the way it goes day in, day out. Week after week, month after month, year after year. But in December 1941, it all ends because of the Japanese attack on Pearl Harbor and Roosevelt's executive order, which sweeps up Wataru and Koto. Their property is confiscated, their business is closed, and the couple is deported to the Manzanar War Relocation Center. When they arrive, there is still desert all around them, but to their astonishment they see tips of wheat sprouting from the ground directly in front of the camp, with long rows of seedlings lined up next to them. It seems that those who came to Manzanar before them have already set to work. People say that the gardeners from Los Angeles have found a new purpose in the middle of the Sierra Nevada.

Over the course of 1942, the desert town of Manzanar becomes a grotesque oasis. Soon after the arrival of the first Japanese, the barren land outside the camp gates is cultivated. Shrubs are cleared and rocks are removed from the grounds. Then the soil is plowed, irrigated, sown, or planted—a total of 440 acres full of potatoes, grain and beets, tomatoes, cucumbers and beans, radishes, carrots and onions, pumpkins, melons, and whatever else the belly may crave.

But that's not all, because what happens outside the camp perimeter on a large scale is continued inside the camp, only on a smaller and more refined scale, and wherever they are granted permission, the internees lay out beds, ornamental gardens, and even small parks. And permission is granted almost everywhere. Gardens are even placed in the narrow spaces between the barracks, in the firebreaks—the internees conjure up what they call "victory gardens."

It's as if history is mirroring itself. But maybe history is just trying to reach the same goal from another direction, who knows … But one thing is certain: while 240 miles away in Pacific Palisades the fire brigade digs up the land for the people to grow lettuce, potatoes, and cucumbers, and demonstrates the right way to create firebreaks against

Japanese bombs, the Japanese in Manzanar are digging up firebreaks and building their own gardens on them.

The result: within half a year, not only has Manzanar become self-sufficient, but the inmates have regained their self-confidence, and it doesn't take long before schools, libraries, and shops are set up in Manzanar; sports fields, leisure facilities, and a Buddhist temple are built; and a police station, a hospital, and even a textile factory, with hundreds of sewing machines rattling about from dawn to dusk, are all established.

And Wataru and Koto? They live right in the middle of it all, in Block 22, Building 9, Room 4—and nobody takes any notice of them.
It seems that nobody has any recollection of them. And they haven't left a trace anywhere else. The camp newspaper, which reports on every little incident and names thousands of inmates for three and a half years, doesn't mention Wataru and Koto Shimidzu even once. Nor do any of Manzanar's numerous photographic collections—which, in contrast to Thomas Mann's diaries, mention the complete names of those pictured—feature Mr. and Mrs. Shimidzu anywhere.

It is as though Wataru and Koto had never been to Manzanar, and no matter which archive I consult, through which collection I search, and whatever search engine I use, there is nothing of Wataru and Koto Shimidzu except a single file telling me that they lived in the camp from June 1, 1942 to September 30, 1945, in Block 22, Building 9, Room 4.

What is to be done, then? I am 240 miles away from a solution and have neither a plan of action nor a hypothesis, because I simply don't know what happened to the two in Manzanar, nor can I say how they ended up in Thomas Mann's house. I basically know almost nothing about Wataru and Koto Shimidzu—until, yes, until I have an idea …

Strictly speaking, it's less of an idea than a hunch derived from my own research experience. It tells me that Thomas Mann gave me the wrong name with "Vattaru," which I corrected to eventually find the right persons. And so I wonder why this approach shouldn't work the other way around? Now that I have the correct name, why shouldn't I look for the wrong one? And why not change the surname instead of the first name?

In other words, if I want to know what Wataru and Koto did before their time with Thomas Mann, I have to take a page out of Thomas Mann's book and find my own luck in misspellings.

Because I don't know how to transcribe Japanese names correctly and have no desire to familiarize myself with the standard ISO 3602 "Romanization of Japanese," I simply try out every possible (and perhaps every impossible) spelling. After four days of searching in vain, I come across the memoirs of a certain Mitsue Nishio, which I read only to be able to confirm to myself that my misspelling hunch was by far the worst idea I could have had. And thus I learn that Mrs. Nishio was born in Seattle in 1917, that she came to Manzanar in April 1942 and was interned there until December 1945, that she got married in the camp, gave birth to a son and made friends—and that two of these friends were called Wataru and Koto Shimizu. "They were my neighbors," she says.

There it is, the misspelling, an omitted "d" in the surname, a laughable and barely perceptible gap that cost me four days of work and still led me to my objective—an objective I would never have reached along the "right" path.

And thus I reassure myself that my search for misspellings was by far the best idea I could have had, while Mitsue Nishio continues telling me about Wataru Shimidzu …

XVII

"He was a businessman before he went to camp. After he came out the camp there's no business there, so he became a gardener like everybody else did."

"A gardener like everybody else": considering the story I'm trying to tell, nothing could be more unsuitable. Then again, perhaps it fits much better than I think, perhaps in the search for misspellings not only will the journeys become the rewards but the rewards themselves will be transformed. I don't know. But it doesn't bother me, because it looks as though I have indeed found Thomas Mann's next gardener after Ted Löwenstein.

The only thing I still need is an answer to the question of how Wataru and Koto ended up in Thomas Mann's house and garden. There is nothing in Mitsue Nishio's report about this, but through a series of detours, I learn that she is still alive, just like her camp-born son, and I decide to contact them both.

I am lucky that even as a centenarian Mitsue Nishio still has a good memory, and that her son Alan is a great admirer of Thomas Mann, as he tells me in his reply. They don't know how Wataru and Koto came to the house on San Remo Drive, but they tell me that Wataru worked as a guard in the camp and helped out Koto in the canteen of Block 22. I learn that they were friendly but very quiet people and only moved to Block 22 when, after some time, a room become vacant there. But the move led to more than just a change of location in the camp, because Block 22 was known for planning a very special garden, and it didn't take long before Wataru and Koto became a part of that plan and helped in its execution. When it was completed, Block 22 had a garden right in front of the canteen. There was a good reason for this, as the cook of Block 22 was known for his outstanding food. People would gather in front of the canteen long before mealtimes. And the garden they planted wasn't just a simple green area with a few flower beds, but an authentic Japanese garden in the traditional style, with water features, stone formations, a pond, and even a traditional wishing well.

This exquisite garden was given the name Three Sack Pond because the camp administration provided each block with three sacks of cement per month for embellishment measures — and Block 22 had decided to use theirs to build a pond that was typical of Japanese ornamental gardens.

When the work was completed, people sat on the stones around the pond, looked at the wishing well that made them feel like they were in a real Japanese garden, and waited for the gong to call them to dinner. This routine only changed once, in December 1942, when there was a violent disturbance in Manzanar. It started in Block 22, of all places, where Wataru was assigned as a security guard and Koto worked in the kitchen, where the friendly and quiet couple Shimidzu lived, in the garden in front of the canteen, where the only revolt Manzanar ever experienced began. When the dust settled, nine internees were injured — and a seventeen-year-old boy was dead.

Perhaps it was this day that was responsible for the fear Koto Shimidzu carried in her, which would later cause her to collapse again and again in Thomas Mann's house — that fear in which Thomas Mann saw little more than the nervous disposition of a "hysterical" woman who would then suddenly be unable to work, which was always "very inconvenient" for the master of the house.

So who were they, Koto and Wataru Shimidzu?

Was she a quiet, reserved, middle-aged lady, or a nervous, hysterical woman?

What about him? Did he help quell the uprising as a security guard, or did he take the side of the insurgent internees? Or did he keep out of the fighting, reserved and calm, as was his nature according to those who lived with him in the camp?

To tell you the truth, I don't know. And how could I? The image of a person is shaped by the perception of others. And as one gets closer to this person, this image is refracted; it is transformed or even replaced. This applies to everyone, but especially to those who leave an abundance of historical traces …

When Koto and Wataru Shimidzu assume their duties in Thomas Mann's house on October 4, 1945, they have no idea who the elderly gentleman standing before them is. All they know is that it's only been five days since they left the camp — and that this must suffice to turn the cook Koto and the guard Wataru into a housekeeper and a gardener.

When the Tail Wags the Dog,
Love Is in the Air

It's a strange feeling to be back at San Remo Drive and recount episodes from Thomas Mann's life. I had moved away from him, and I enjoyed the distance. But now he is back — and with him the staccato of his diary entries.

10.05.1945: "The Japanese couple is serving."
10.06.1945: "The Japanese couple quite touching and industrious."

But Thomas Mann was also touching and industrious. When I had left him, over three years ago, in July 1942, he sat in his living room reading magazines. He was happy with his house.

The only thing that didn't go the way he wanted was the domestic staff. But since then a lot has happened. The war is over, Hitler has been defeated, and the domestic-staff crisis seems to have found its solution in Koto and Wataru — and even if Thomas Mann is now free to return to Germany, he doesn't return. And that's not just because he doesn't want to. He has taken root on the little hill where the house stands. Since June 21, 1943, the stationery lying on the desk in his study has carried the address of San Remo Drive. Ever since that day, every letter of his to Germany is officially a letter to a foreign country, written by someone who has been an American citizen since June 1944. And the end of the war doesn't change anything. When Thomas Mann learns of the German surrender, he is convinced that the victory is due above all to America and President Roosevelt, who died shortly before the end of the war.

He himself survived. That's all. For the time being, this victory is purely physical in nature — on the inside, Thomas Mann is "not exactly elated" when he learns of the final defeat of Hitler's Germany.

The way back remains cut off. His own roots may only reach into the upper layers of the Californian soil, but the fangs of National Socialism have penetrated deep into the subsoil of Germany, and the entire country is infested with its evil spirit from head to toe. To return to it would mean to become a member of the community of shattered existences. For someone like Thomas Mann, this isn't an option, especially when the sun is shining here in California, when he lives in the most beautiful house he has ever owned, and when his literary fame is greater than ever before—after all, he is considered "the greatest living man of letters" in America. The fact that many in Germany are pleading for his return doesn't change this. They worship him. They call him. They reach out their hands to him. But he does not return. As a result, he is publicly reviled, he is accused of arrogance, ignorance, and a lack of love for his fatherland, and doubts are raised whether he is still "a part of German literature"—which is, of course, just one more reason to stay in California and let his roots here grow a little deeper.

"Plan to buy a small private beach to work and rest in the summer," the diary says in May 1945.
This plan, however, will never be implemented, because the Californian coast is neither a place of work nor rest for Thomas Mann ...

09.13.1945: "At noon excursion with the children to a more distant beach. Lunch in the sand. Beautiful surf, seagulls, sandpipers and jumping sand fleas. Bad for shoes and clothes."

09.14.1945: "Slept badly, got a cold and was overexcited. Eripal + Jyrab calcium + cough mixture. Shoes and suit for cleaning. Never again—the beach trip."

His excursions thereafter resume in the form of walks. They are undertaken alone rather than with the family and do not lead to any distant beach, but one and a half miles down the road to Amalfi Drive, directly to the house that the family rented until February 1942 — a small remnant from earlier times, while another remnant from the past has disappeared altogether.

On Monday, May 21, 1945, Thomas Mann throws his diaries from 1921–33 into the flames of the oven in the garden. It is not the first time he has incinerated records of his own life. Already, in June 1944, a few days before he became an American citizen, he had burned several diaries. Now, two weeks after the German surrender, he brings the matter to an end and hauls the "piles of paper" out of the study into the garden. Into the oven. Into the fire. Into oblivion. Even if, in this case, it is not his personal memory that he erases, but merely the prospect of someone who survives him trying to weave their own stories from this raw material of history.

And while one is wiped out, the other is renewed. In July 1945 the villa on San Remo Drive is given a new coat of paint, and inside, in the rooms, the painters and decorators are at work as well. And yet it seems that in this case, too, the renewal is connected with one's own life and has less to do with the corrosions of the Californian climate than with the convulsions of German history. Two months earlier, Thomas Mann learned from his son Klaus, who was staying in Munich, that their former house in Poschingerstrasse had been hit during the bombardment and was seriously damaged both inside and out. Shortly afterward, Thomas Mann commissioned the Californian villa to be repainted.

Is all the painting just a form of aesthetic compensation? A dash of color amid the grey clouds that rise in the east and cast their shadows all the way to distant America? Or is it not connected to any of this, is it perhaps just a signal shining from the Californian hills that someone is experiencing his second spring here in this first postwar summer?

To be honest, I don't know, but it doesn't matter because I'm not interested in psychologizing literature or literati; I prefer to stick to tangible things. And here we see that even after seven years in America, Thomas Mann still knows nothing about money, because he doesn't measure the cost of painting in dollars, but in manuscript pages: "This will take the entire commission for the Dostoevsky essay," he complains, while the painters swing their brushes in the blazing heat of the Californian summer and Thomas Mann has to continue writing on the terrace, as the ceiling in his study also gets a new coat of paint.

After ten days everything is as new again, the gang of painters has disappeared, and Thomas Mann is happy about his villa shining in the sun. And everything around the house is fresh as well; the beauty is almost tangible.
The plot of land, which was a little neglected due to the conscription of the "gardener" Golo, soon presents itself in all its splendor again. Only a few weeks after Wataru began his service, the overgrown borders and flowerbeds have disappeared, the flowers are in bloom, the vegetables are flourishing, and the lawn that had been burned by the sun is beginning to turn green again. Even the shrubs and trees have been pruned.

From now on, the garden and villa will outshine each other—and the green thumbs from Japan conduct their work just as successfully inside the house. Koto decorates the rooms with fresh flowers and creates ornate still lifes from twigs, stones, and berries.

And yet even on the day of their arrival, there are already problems. Not with them, however, but with Niko, the French poodle …

On the day Wataru and Koto start their service, the dog has disappeared once again, which is why Thomas Mann has no choice but to place a notice in the newspaper to look for him. It is not known what the notice says—we can only hope that Thomas Mann didn't just write "Poodle escaped," because the animal doesn't look like a cute little white poodle at all. It is burly and black and at present probably battered and bruised.

The fact that the animal should be on the loose in such a dreadful state and not find its way home is due to a series of failed amorous advances, but this is no reason for the poodle not to jump headlong into the next tryst.

That Niko won't just encounter other dogs on his forays but also coyotes, who live on the still-undeveloped hills west of San Remo Drive and descend in droves at night, is just the nature of things, or a thing of nature—just as it is Thomas Mann's habit to make contact with his neighbors through Niko, even if he may think less of most of his contemporaries than he does of a randy poodle. As a consequence, these encounters are often irate exchanges with the owners of bitches in heat, and the only one with whom Thomas Mann maintains a friendly relationship because of his dog is Lester Ziffren, "his good nabour" from across the street.

Ziffren is actually a reporter and had a coup in 1936 when, despite interrupted communication links and cut-off telephone lines, he succeeded in breaking news of the impending Spanish Civil War to the world on July 17 by sending an inconspicuous telegram from Madrid to his news agency in London. The seemingly trivial text was an acrostic, spelling out the words "Melilla foreign legion revolted martial law declared."

Six years later, it is Thomas Mann who writes a few inconspicuous words that don't make for good English but do serve as an expression of gratitude. When the Mann family travels or goes out for the night,

XVIII

Lester Ziffren always steps in as a "dog-sitter." And so it happens that the very same Lester Ziffren, who now works as a scriptwriter in Hollywood, no longer takes the Spanish military censor for a ride but Thomas Mann's poodle for a walk.

Even he, however, can't prevent the animal from running off again and again, and when Niko still isn't back on the evening of October 4, everyone is prepared for the worst.

"With every hour that passes, safe return more unlikely," Thomas Mann notes in his diary. He's sad. He is attached to the poodle ("I loved him at first sight"), even if the animal sometimes drives him crazy, which is not surprising since the French pedigree is bred for "Gueulard," meaning "Big Mouth," and the dog's coat resembles Louis XIV's hair.

At least that's the verdict of the author Aldous Huxley, who lives not far from San Remo Drive, while Thomas Mann himself likens Niko to "an Ethiopian prince," at least when he's freshly coiffed rather than freshly crumpled.

But now Niko has disappeared, and Thomas Mann sits alone in his study on the evening of October 4. He wants to read a little, but he simply cannot focus and fails to classify the events unfolding in front of him into the familiar categories of reality and illusion. When he puts his book down, nothing remains but doubts, questions, and entanglements that he, Thomas Mann, can't get his head around. It is—as he calls it—"the non-novelistic, strangely real biographical quality that is nonetheless fiction."

After he has noted his thoughts, Thomas Mann leaves the study, climbs up his private stairs to the sleeping chamber, and goes to bed. When he wakes up the next morning, the poodle sends him a sign of life from Beverly Hills, seven miles away.

Wataru retrieves the dog by car.

Then he collects another passenger, a woman named Katzenellenbogen, a Jewish surname that originates from an eponymous town in
the Rhineland but literally translates from German as "cat's elbow." As
requested by Thomas Mann, Wataru takes both to San Remo Drive.

The master of the house wants to lunch with one of them and punch
the other.

Luckily, he only gets halfway through this list.

The next day the animal confusion continues. Wataru observes Thomas Mann as he is reading a book with cat stories. A short time later
the master of the house tells him that after his walk he had been collected by a little dog called Hallgarten. The poodle doesn't seem to
be involved. The confusion seems to have spread from animals to
humans. The entanglements increase. There is consternation.

On October 31, Wataru drives Mrs. Katzenellenbogen home after the
lunch. On the evening of that same day, Thomas Mann finds "broken glass and garbage in the yard."

On November 20, the Nuremberg trials open in Germany. In Pacific
Palisades, the wind blows "landward after dinner," whereupon
Thomas Mann feels "poorly and tired."

On December 5, Thomas Mann receives a letter from Argentina.
The sender implores him never to return to Germany. A few hours
later Thomas Mann visits the philosopher Theodor W. Adorno, who
lives not far from him. Adorno reads to Thomas Mann from his book
of aphorisms. To Thomas Mann, the words seem "devastating and
sad."

On January 7, there is a "great conflagration moving uphill" west of San Remo Drive. The sight of the flames leaves Thomas Mann shaken.

On February 18, just a few miles from San Remo Drive, a young man bludgeons a lawyer to death on the open road with an iron pipe. Both parties are barely clothed at the time. Thomas Mann tries to comprehend the murderous rage that sometimes befalls closeted homosexual men after intercourse, but doesn't come to a conclusion.

On March 1, Thomas Mann and his wife are invited to dinner by the writer Franz Werfel. On the way back they get lost with the car in dense fog. Meanwhile, he receives all sorts of "repulsive" documents from Germany, declaring him a traitor to the fatherland. Thomas Mann's first thought: "Make no more statements, give them no more ammunition."

A few weeks later, on April 11, 1946, Koto and Wataru stand at the door, stunned. Thomas Mann is carried out of the house on a stretcher.

His lung is cancerous, only Thomas Mann doesn't know that, and if (and because) his wife Katia has her way, he never will know. He is simply suffering from an infected abscess in his lungs, absolutely benign, not worrisome at all.

The surgery in Chicago goes without complications. The subsequent recovery is going well.
Thomas Mann's insouciance, born of his blissful ignorance, also plays its part.

I'll play my part and try to do a little more research on Mann's medical history. In the official journal of the German Medical Association, I find an essay from 2016 on Mann's surgery, but contrary to my expectations its findings are historical rather histological.

"A Successful Lung Operation on Thomas Mann 70 Years Ago and Its Significance for the Culture of Central Germany" is the title of this treatise. It suggests the following hypothesis: had Thomas Mann died during the operation, it would have been a bitter loss for the culture of this region, since he would not have finished his novel *Doctor Faustus* and thus nobody would have learned that the protagonist's home village and early stomping grounds were all in Central Germany.

After I put down the essay, I feel as if neither the fictions of a novel nor those of a biography could be declared either reality or illusion, and I get the feeling — in view of Thomas Mann, the Medical Association's journal, and my own health — that it would be better if I left Thomas Mann in the hospital in Chicago for another while, put the newspaper away, and got some fresh air.

When I step outside, I see that it's autumn. The trees spread their bare branches into the sky, and the grazing sheep stare at me as if we had changed roles. Behind them, on the meadow, someone has swept the tin leaves into a rusty pile.
Thinking, I think, has transformed the landscape. Or maybe it has just fulfilled it. I don't know. I'm standing in a meadow that belongs to me. Between two sheep I raised. In front of the pile of leaves that I raked up last night. I am standing in a small village, somewhere in Central Germany. Winter is slowly beginning to set in. California, I think to myself, California is an option …

On May 27, 1946, Thomas Mann is back home. For six weeks he hasn't see San Remo Drive. Koto looked after the house, and Wataru has done a great job in the garden. "Enchanted by the light, by the colours. Garden and view heavenly," Thomas Mann notes in his diary on May 28 — and he cannot stop enthusing over the following days.

05.29.1946: "Walk in the garden, delightful."

05.30.1946: "In and out of the garden, which looks incredibly splendid and luminous."

06.01.1946: "Once more joy in the beauty of the garden."

06.09.1946: "Walk around in the garden, which is abundant with flowers." And because it wasn't cancer officially, but only a small abscess: "I can afford half a cigar after dinner again."

Everything remains unchanged. Apart from one thing. Since the operation, Thomas Mann has been troubled by back pain, which makes it impossible for him to continue sitting at his desk, but he soon finds a new place in his study and from then on makes himself at home on the flowery sofa Paul Huldschinsky brought with him from Beverly Hills. Thomas Mann continues to write into a notebook on his knees, and the sofa gives him the grounding he needs for his work to grow in peace.

And just as ink fuses with paper, so Thomas Mann grows with the sofa. So much so that he takes it with him to Switzerland when he leaves America years later. The returnee cannot live without the sofa in his new home. Unfortunately, there is no room for the sofa in his new home. And so it is no wonder that Thomas Mann soon reports attacks of acute pain and fills the pages of his diary again and again with the same sad lamentations. "I miss the sofa corner of my room in P.P.," he writes in plaintive prose.

It takes until April 15, 1954, for Thomas Mann to be able to use his beloved item of furniture once again. "Touching motion, sitting before and after tables on my P.P. sofa again," he writes in his diary, and it seems as if the sofa reminds him that he was once there, in America, and that he was contented, in his little corner, somewhere back there, in California …

But now, in June 1946, what will one day be nostalgic stands before him in all its magnificence — the sofa, the study, his large, luminous, lovely Californian home.

"Brightest weather, dazzling flowers," it says in his diary on June 23, and the next morning also looks like a picture postcard: blue skies, sunshine, and breakfast on the terrace.

But then, on June 26: "Burst pipe in the garden."

This is followed by a servant crisis ("Koto melancholic-hysteric"), a power failure ("Niko causes a short by pulling down the night lamp, to his great consternation"), a group of literature scholars ("foolish"), and a lizard wandering into the living room where it is spellbound by the painting of an old German master ("expedited into the garden by Vattaru").

Shortly after, Koto and Wataru leave the house.

The day of their departure is not mentioned by Thomas Mann and on August 12, 1946, he merely reports the "engagement of a Negro domestic service couple" who will start work the following morning.

From time to time, Koto and Wataru will return to help in the garden or the kitchen or to look after the house when the Manns are out of town, but their presence will now always have the character of a visit.

According to Thomas Mann, they went "to stand on their own feet," but if there is any truth in that, it's only half the story, because Koto is sick. Their years in the camp have taken their toll, and working in the Mann house also became more and more of a burden, especially since dealing with the family was not always easy and complaints about Koto's "lapses" had grown more frequent. And so Koto and Wataru left the house. But they didn't return to their old lives. The gates of their former fruit and vegetable wholesale store remain closed forever, and they don't consider the possibility of opening their own nursery either. Instead, Koto and Wataru go to Sawtelle, a district in west LA where a large Japanese community has lived since the turn of the century and is slowly coming back to life after the war and the end of the internment.

From now on, however, they are in the service of the West Los Angeles United Methodist Church. Here, only half a mile from their small apartment on South Westgate Avenue, they get involved in this church that was established by Japanese immigrants. They organize events and will soon conduct their own church services.

It is the story of a late blooming, but one that will endure for decades, until the end.

Wataru Shimidzu will die on February 21, 1992. Koto will follow him only a few months later, on October 2, almost forty-seven years to the day since Thomas Mann announced the "entry of a Japanese domestic service couple" in his diary.

Slowly Losing Touch with Polite Society and Growing Old with a Gentle Sigh

Should any mortal ever find the energy (or some immortal soul ever find the inclination, out of pure boredom) to scour thousands of diary entries, countless books and letters, and piles of papers in order to establish the number of people who made their way to San Remo Drive by car, bus, or bicycle between 1942 and 1952 to visit Thomas Mann, they would probably arrive at a figure close to ten thousand. And this is not only because Thomas Mann is the uncrowned king of exile whom everyone asks for advice, opinions, and help, but also because his address and number are listed in the telephone directory. Just call 54403, make an appointment, and you can meet the famous writer.

And they all come:
Associates, buddies, and carpetbaggers,
Committee delegates, emigrant braggers,
Finicky Germans and hoi poloi,
Interviewers who come to annoy,
Journalists, judges, and killers-with-kindness,
Liberal thinkers lamenting behindness,
Movie moguls and mental migrators,
Narcistic nincompoops, other orators,
Orchestra players and plump politicians,
Queasy quacks and readers on missions,
Reds-under-beds and spoilt sons with their pops,
Schmucks and schlimazels and schlemiels and fops,
Tradesmen with trowels and unfaithful youth,
Vansittartists, vendors of vermouth,
Warriors, worriers, Washington wags,
Xenophobes, X-troverts, quixotic stags,
Yearners and earners and Yale PhDs,
Yawners and dawners and X, Y, and Zs.

XIX

They all come, ring the doorbell, and meet a maid who opens the door for them but doesn't let them in while she reaches silently for the cards that are handed to her or remembers the names of the visitors who then wait outside the door … and wait … and wait … until the maid returns and bids them to enter ("Step in").

You step into a small lobby, take off your coat and hat, and are asked to proceed ("Go ahead").

In front of you, you see a large double door, one side slightly ajar, and you knock.

"If you please," a voice sounds from the other side, and you enter the living room.

Katia Mann comes forward with short, nimble steps, and she intercepts you while Thomas Mann rises slowly from his armchair behind her. He wears white shoes and a grey suit. A short handshake, a somewhat formal greeting, then he sits down again. You sit down on the chair offered to you. Katia takes the chair in between. The only way to her husband, that much is clear, is through her. He talks. She listens to what you have to say.

The conversation flows, a gentle breeze of words. Platitudes, compliments, banalities.

Ten minutes. Mann talks.
Twenty minutes. Mann listens.
Thirty minutes. One talks.
Forty minutes. One still listens.
Fifty minutes, and she starts getting restless. She doesn't say a word, but you can tell that enough has been said.
You get up, she's up just as fast.
He follows suit a moment later.
A handshake. She accompanies you to the door while Thomas Mann slowly sinks back into his armchair …

Quite a few visitors report that they were disappointed by their conversations with Thomas Mann. There are no big speeches, no pithy witticisms, no sweeping debates. Instead, there are well-tempered chats that take place several times a week in the living room. Sixty minutes in which the epic gives way to the ephemeral. And why not? Thomas Mann is neither a party animal nor a great orator; he is someone who writes into silence. To him, the "kneading" of his thoughts is as contemplative as it is lonely, something that belongs in his study rather than the parlor.

Still, they all come, for years, but the many visitors are not the only ones who fill the house on San Remo Drive. There are also the six children who often stay in the house for weeks, sometimes even months; the grandchildren and Thomas Mann's brother Heinrich; not to forget the friends and acquaintances who are invited to dinner or one of the usual émigré parties.

It is no wonder that Thomas Mann took precautions during the planning phase and created his own little kingdom in the form of his study. From an architectural point of view, the room constitutes its own structure, which has the shape of a cube and reveals itself as a kind of appendage to the house, only this appendage isn't hidden at the back, but protrudes from the façade, clearly visible to everyone—a characteristic that would actually attract curious glances if it wasn't for the wall running straight from the study into the garden, twelve feet long by seven feet high, a kind of appendage to the appendage that ensures that nobody becomes too attached.

But inside the villa, there is also peace and quiet, since the kitchen, laundry room, and maid's room are on the other side of the house, a good hundred feet from the study, and even the living room is separated from the writing room by a heavy door.

"It was quite closed off," Thomas Mann's daughter Monika will explain decades later on a visit to the house. She is not talking about the study, however, but rather the maid's room, yet the closed-offness basically applies to both of them, the distance of one determining the other's detachment. But there is something else because between the study and the maid's room lie the public rooms of the family, the dining and living rooms, along with the large terrace in front of them. They form a kind of buffer between Thomas Mann's working environment and that of his servants.

And yet these public spaces must also be delineated, both in one direction and the other.

This is easy in the case of the study because Davidson designed the house in such a way that the study faces west—i.e., toward the terrace—and has no windows but a heavy door that ensures tranquility and order inside.

It is more difficult, however, to separate the public rooms from the utility wing and the maid's room. Although distinctive floor coverings, furnishings, and room sizes clearly demarcate the different spheres within the house, it is not so easy to separate them from the outside. The desire for differentiation can only be fulfilled long after the house has been completed, even though the terrace in front of the living and dining rooms immediately reveals the difference, and their walled enclosure and elevated location distinguish it visibly from the world of domestic work and the rooms of domestic workers.

And yet in the end, it is left to a hedge several yards high to make the full extent of the difference visible. It was planted around the utility wing in 1942 and over the years would grow into a veritable wall behind which the maid's room, the laundry room, and the storage room for the garden tools disappeared in diametrical relation to the terrace and the rooms of the family behind it, which opened up to the eye of the onlooker.

"There was always this sense of class consciousness," Monika Mann would say on her last visit to the house, and I realize that this class consciousness, this vertical stratification of life, was implemented spatially on San Remo Drive, on a single level.

Thomas Mann's study, on the other hand, is quite a different matter. The wall does not rise in front of the window but runs from the side of the room out into the garden, which is why rather than acting as an obstacle it opens up the view for the room's occupant while simultaneously protecting him from curious onlookers. And if that's not enough, there are still the venetian blinds inside the room — miniature plastic walls that can be opened and closed in no time at all, just the way Mann likes it.

And thus the study reveals itself not only as the most prominent part of the entire building, but also as a poet's dungeon of sorts. A turret room on the ground floor. A monastic cell surrounded by palm trees — with a bottle of Cinzano on the table.

And yet even a poet must leave his dungeon. Especially when his family throws a party and its guests are already waiting in the living room.

And so it happens that on the evening of August 24, 1946, Thomas Mann enters the living room a little grumpy — the imminent celebration has prevented him from finishing a letter — and pays his respects to the exiles waiting there. All of German California, it seems, has gathered in his villa, and instead of tending to cultured correspondence, he has to join the fray at the buffet table. After a while, Thomas Mann has had his fill of canapés, small talk, and stories from the past. Around eleven o'clock he retreats into his study and then retires up his private stairs to the bedroom, while downstairs they'll party on and make noise until two o'clock.

The next morning there is a big mess, the staff is late, and a team of *Life* magazine photographers is roaming the house. Because Thomas Mann has not yet surfaced, they start by photographing the interior and then the garden.

When Thomas Mann finally arrives, he is photographed all over the house. The pack of photographers even follows him on his walk and keeps snapping during lunch.

Thomas Mann is glad that he invited Adorno over today, as this will allow him to return to his study immediately after lunch and spend the following hours discussing the philosopher's aphorisms. That these are of a downright devastating melancholy does not matter. In view of the photographers who are still rummaging about all over the house, even deeply sad aphorisms are a comfort for Thomas Mann.

When he returns to the living room around half past five, the photographers are still there. But his daughter Erika and his sons Klaus and Golo have made themselves comfortable in the house. The result: "Living Room a mess, interminable photo session, between it all the children …"

The next day Thomas Mann finds a box of chocolates at his front door. It was put there by Florence Homolka. She is the daughter of his patron Agnes Meyer, but among the émigrés of Pacific Palisades she is mainly known as a photographer, and it looks like Thomas Mann is supposed to be her model again. But first of all, there are chocolates and an invitation which is attached to the box. It says that the next dinner party will take place tonight, just a few houses away from San Remo Drive …

What's that? Is life in Californian exile like a box of chocolates? A smorgasbord of delicacies where you never know exactly what you'll get, but where you can be sure that—if you open it in the evening after work—a few chocolates will definitely be the reward of the day? Is this what exile in America looks like? Are these the oft-mentioned stall-and-circle seats from which the émigrés watch the German tragedy at a safe distance? Is this place the real paradise, and its real name Pacific Praline-ades?

The image emerging from the letters and diaries of émigrés who live in the hills west of Los Angeles is deceptive, for it is all too easy to get the impression that the time of exile consists to no small extent of evening parties, salon conversations, and reciprocal tea invitations. The reality is somewhat different: it is, unsurprisingly, much more quotidian, common, and casual. Even where one dinner party chases the next, from at least 1946 on an imminent farewell is secretly celebrating itself.

And it has every reason to do so. The wartime restrictions and curfews have lifted, and distance becomes a matter of choice again. It doesn't take long for the first émigrés to turn their backs on California and return to Germany. Hitler united them, and now they part company again.

Some return because they have never really found their bearings in America; others because they miss their fatherland, their mother tongue, the childhood dreams they have contrived in old age; while yet others believe that they can only rehabilitate themselves professionally and socially in Germany—old contacts, new happiness, why should fate be a one-way street?

It is a slow sapping of the émigré community, an imperceptible drifting apart, although the new distance is by no means always an entire ocean. Even within America, in California and even in LA, many émi-grés reinvent and reposition themselves—geographically, commer-cially, and sometimes also intellectually and politically. But that's not all, because the American government is also repositioning itself.

The Committee for Un-American Activities, which dedicated itself to counteracting fascist activities in 1934, has already identified a new adversary in December of 1941. From now on it does not fight Nazis anymore but Communists, or rather anyone it deems to be a Communist—and quite a few of whom are German émigrés.

At first glance, it seems paradoxical that this reorientation should take place as early as the end of 1941, directly following the German dec-laration of war against America and the deployment of American troops, but the shift from the (imaginary) Nazi threat to the (imagi-nary) Communist threat is mainly due to internal factors. At a time when millions of Americans serve on foreign battlefields far away from home, the Committee for Un-American Activities has deter-mined the main enemy to come from within, in the shape of the ev-er-stronger trade unions and the New Deal–making President Roo-sevelt, who is fervently revered by Thomas Mann.

By May 1945, at the latest, when Roosevelt is dead and Germany defeated, anti-Communism can unleash its full force in America.

When the Republicans finally win the congressional elections in No-vember 1946 and thus take over the chair of the House Committee for Un-American Activities, the time comes for open denunciations, intimidation, and persecution.

And while (and because) the anti-Communist exorcists are on the ram-page around Hollywood, in particular, more and more German émi-grés are put on the blacklists that were created for the alleged Reds.

It's the same as ever: the scope of one's power and the size of the imagined threat are directly correlated, and wherever one grows, the other grows with it. As power expands, it feeds on the images it has created, and finally begins to disembowel its own political culture.

And so it happens that the little Weimar Republic that the German exiles had carefully nurtured under the Californian palm trees is slowly disintegrating—is being corroded from the outside and at the same time from within—and when in May 1947 local newspaper the *Palisadian* proudly presents its readers with a list of more than sixty well-known personalities living in Pacific Palisades, the once-large German émigré community of artists and scientists has shrunk to the two writers Lion Feuchtwanger and Thomas Mann, the latter tellingly referred to as "one of America's greatest novelists."

Certainly, that's just a reporter's point of view, and Pacific Palisades—just like Santa Monica, Westwood, or Bel Air—is still home to many German émigrés who at this time are only beginning to leave the country, or are indeed staying, as many do as well. And yet the inner and outer disintegration of the émigré community after 1947 can no longer be overlooked.

But there is something else that shrinks the émigré community and tears at its very fabric—and that is death. On June 20, 1945, one of Thomas Mann's closest friends in exile, the writer Bruno Frank, dies in his house in Beverly Hills. Only two months later, on August 26, Franz Werfel passes away. Shortly thereafter, on September 26, he is followed by the playwright Richard Beer-Hofmann, who had visited Thomas Mann in Princeton in 1940 and whose book *Jacob's Dream* had inspired Thomas Mann's exploration of the biblical material from which the *Joseph* novels would later emerge. Beer-Hofmann's book had made a "big impression" on Mann, and even though the former lived in Vienna and later in exile in New York, Mann had called him

a friend and asked about his well-being on several occasions. But now he was dead. And some of those who still remained soon wanted to leave the country and return to Germany.

"The circle of friends is dying out, it is getting lonely," Thomas Mann had already stated in 1945, and in this way, his summary at the end of the year was more than understandable. "What a good time was the war!" he bemoaned to a friend. "Deceptively good …"

The picture drawn by Paul Huldschinsky in 1945 is also deceptively good. After all, he's won an Oscar, his business is going well, and he is still a welcome guest in Thomas Mann's house, bringing old furniture with him, hanging up new paintings, or simply stopping by for tea. And yet something has changed because Paul Huldschinsky has cancer. Unlike Thomas Mann, however, he does know about it — but his cancer is inoperable.

When Paul Huldschinsky stops by for dinner in July 1946, Thomas Mann is shocked. "Emaciated appearance," he notes in his diary. Half a year later, Paul Huldschinsky is dead. He dies on February 1, 1947, a day when the weather forecast reports warm and dry descending air currents.

Thomas Mann expresses his condolences by letter.
His wife attends the funeral.
The weather gets worse.

02.06.1947: "Overcast and cool."
02.07.1947: "Heavy fog, very cool."
02.08.1947: "Fog."
02.09.1947: "Extraordinarily dark. Days of rain announced."

When spring finally returns to California, Thomas Mann leaves San Remo Drive and travels to Europe.

On May 10, 1947, he boards the RMS *Queen Elizabeth* in New York to travel to London. It's the first time in nine years that he's returned to the Old World. He stays three months, visiting England, Switzerland, and the Netherlands. He does not go to Germany, although special emissaries are sent to Zurich to persuade him to visit his homeland. Or what they take to be his homeland. But Thomas Mann has taken precautions: "Discussion with the general, who is supposed to *not* grant us entry to Germany."

And where there's no will, there's no way.

No wonder Thomas Mann notes on his way back to America: "The impatience to return home is great." And then: "I hate the spaces that separate me from the house there and the poodle."

The poodle, that fleabag … For the duration of his vacation, Thomas Mann has placed him in the care of his friend the photographer Ernst Gottlieb, but at the first opportunity the animal escaped to make a few rounds through Pacific Palisades in the hope of an amorous adventure, and finally ran back to San Remo Drive on his own, because no lady dog wanted to cavort with him.

The result: Ernst Gottlieb despaired and assumed the animal to be dead. The servants at San Remo Drive were surprised and happy that they didn't have to retrieve the dog by car this time.

And since everything was as it was, and everyone thought they knew what they were doing, the whole matter remained unresolved — at least until Thomas Mann comes home, wonders about the presence of the poodle, and can do nothing but apologize to Ernst Gottlieb for the chaos caused by the dog and ask him to "deliver the ungrateful creature's bed and bowls back to his residence."

The residence, the villa on San Remo Drive … While Thomas Mann was in Europe, the house has filled up with a fearsome jumble of all sorts of documents: letters and books, newspapers and magazines, packages, parcels, and political pamphlets — everything is piled up in the living room on the table, the sofa, the chairs. Even in the corner, on the piano, paper towers are sprouting. This room looks like the mailroom of the Pacific Palisades Post Office.
It will take Thomas Mann many weeks to get the job done.

When he's finished with it, it is not only the paper that has disappeared but also the feeling of home. "I don't know anymore what 'home' really means," he writes to Hermann Hesse in November 1947, and even if he adds that he "basically never knew it," his statement is by no means based on a feeling of eternal rootlessness, but on the nefarious nature of American politics, something that now, in 1947, Thomas Mann experiences first hand.

In March he had already signed an appeal against the Committee for Un-American Activities, then in July he himself had described its activities as un-American, and finally, he had placed the committee members just below Hitler in the list of the people he hated most.

But that's not all. In autumn 1947 Thomas Mann publicly supports the composer Hanns Eisler, who was threatened with deportation for alleged Communist activities, as well as the so-called Hollywood Ten. Yet he never mentions the name of Bertolt Brecht, whom he does not value very much, although he is also summoned before the committee on October 30 and leaves America a day later, never to return. At any rate, there is not a single word about Brecht in the diary for the entire year of 1947. Yet Thomas Mann is clear about the general direction things are going, and in his opinion the further course of history is evident. Fascism, he is certain, will come to America; basically, it is already here.

On October 3, 1947, he notes in his diary, "Horrified by the fading sense of justice in this country, the rule of fascist violence." The deportation of Hanns Eisler, declared to be a voluntary departure, upsets him, even though he rejects the "call to arms," because despite his American citizenship he considers himself to be a guest in this country.

One month later Thomas Mann finally does reveal his thoughts publicly, when he supports a radio program directed against the committee and is happy to "tell these illiterates what he thinks of them" …

Of course, that doesn't change the situation. Certainly, when America hunts down Communists, it overwhelmingly hunts down the wrong people. In essence, it is chasing after its own fears and forcing them deeper and deeper into the country. But this country is Thomas Mann's home, take it or leave it. For nine years and counting.

And Europe? That is far away, and even if he was there only a few months ago, it is "like a dream" to him, one that "I often and gladly follow in my thoughts …"

Europe — the place of longing.
Europe — the exile glorified by the intellect.
Europe — which has left its mark on America.

Europe — "Everything was 'again,'" Thomas Mann writes to Hermann Hesse in November 1947.

But there is no such "again" in America. The return to America was not a return of the intellect, but of the body. And now that the threats have increased and its political culture is reminiscent of Nazi Germany, America is certainly no "again," but rather once more an "against."

And yet Thomas Mann's longing to live again in Europe will remain unspoken for a long time to come. Even in the deeper layers of the diary, in 1947, there is no trace of it—and should there somehow be early murmurs of the desire to return in some back corner of his head, they are drowned out by the usual hustle and bustle of the Mann house.

Books have to be written, letters must be answered, meetings held, visitors received. And then there is the domestic staff—and as always they cause problems …

On November 14, 1947, a new pair of servants are hired and their start is "decent," but they leave the house again after only ten days. Since Thomas Mann can't get by without someone serving the meals—his attempts at serving himself always result in diary entries ("Alone in the house. Prepared tea for myself in the kitchen")—a new domestic-service couple is soon hired: "old Negroes" who are "all too clumsy" and thus three months later will receive a "humane dismissal."

What follows is the "re-engagement of the Felix couple," who had already served on San Remo Drive two years earlier and now return to the house in February 1948. But this is only the beginning of the real problems … Thomas Mann should have known the whole thing wouldn't work—and Katia, who has always been responsible for the servants, even more so. Felix and his wife Joe hadn't been easy to deal with the first time around. Again and again, they had come in late, fought with one another following "marital misunderstandings," or even failed to turn up for work altogether, which was, of course, also due to the fact that Felix was in prison for drunk driving and Joe often went to visit him there.

After their reemployment, the same goes on — jovial indolence, marital conflicts, frequent absences. Only this time Felix refrains from driving under the influence (at least for the time being) and tries his hand at driving without a license instead. Since he doesn't have a car, he takes one from Thomas Mann's son Golo, who is visiting at the moment and in Felix's opinion doesn't need it anyway.

One day later Felix comes back, but rather than show his remorse, "borrows" some money from Thomas Mann.

"Cash theft by Felix. Untenable, which is very unpleasant with the imminent invasion of children and grandchildren," Thomas Mann notes in his diary on June 28, but the chaos will still continue for a while …

07. 09. 1948: "The black domestic service couple out of service, quarrel, drunkenness of the husband."

08. 06. 1948: "I had breakfast in my bedroom, but I am tired of being waited on unwillingly. Made the mistake of complaining about the chocolate mousse."

08. 11. 1948: "End of domestic service couple Joe-Felix, once and for all."

But "once and for all" is one of those things …

08. 14. 1948: "Return of Joe. Her nigger will go to the hospital for serious treatment."

11. 30. 1948: "Felix temporarily arrested."
12. 21. 1948: "No service. Felix sentenced to 60 days, lenient."

But at some point, enough is enough …

03. 28. 1949: "Departure of the blacks, Felix and Joe, due to impossible behavior."

The only question is, Why were Felix and Joe rehired at all? And why did Thomas and Katia Mann keep them in the house for months after the old problems had reappeared? Because they felt sorry for their servants?

I think not. Then because new domestic staff was hard to come by? This was indeed a problem during the war, but things had changed and in the late 1940s there was ample supply on the labor market. Then why? Because every story, however small, must always happen twice, once as tragedy and once as farce? Perhaps. But maybe the reasons are deeper—and maybe this is the moment to take the social-psychological route for a change. It's not that difficult, especially since I don't have to do the bulk of the work myself. I just need to get some relevant studies on the subject; see what they say about the relationship between housewife, master, and servant; and examine the whole thing using the example of the San Remo Drive villa. No big deal, really. A simple comparison, even if I fear that the next chapter will have a somewhat academic touch. But this will just be temporary—and afterward, we'll talk about the weather, I promise …

How to Correctly Articulate Class Consciousness and Still Be Mann Enough as a Woman

The topic "domestic staff of the Mann family" is not exactly a burning issue of Thomas Mann research. The scholarly Germanists have only ever produced platitudes on this matter, and the literary scholars, who are otherwise rarely at a loss for explanations, know nothing about it. As a result, the most detailed account can be found in a book called *If Thomas Mann Were Your Client*, written by a professor of business administration. Here, however, the house on San Remo Drive is only mentioned in passing, and the insights gained are somehow sobering. At the end of the chapter on "Thomas Mann as an Employer," it states: "It is obvious that service managers cannot learn anything directly from Thomas Mann as an employer." In other words, Thomas Mann only serves as a bad example.

What is to be done, then? How can employment relationships on San Remo Drive be investigated without getting bogged down in innocuous examples and irrelevant evaluations? How can the extant anecdotes be harnessed for an exact analysis? And, generally, how can the small picture be integrated into the big one? How can the necessary be combined with the possible?

In such instances, a change of perspective can be the only solution. In this case, that means: get out of Germany, move on to America. Move on from this study of a business-administration professor to the works of feminist historians. In addition to the employment relationships in the Mann household, the focus must also be on the general relationships of work, power, and gender that determined the interaction between heads of household, housewives, and employees—specifically at the time when the family lived in Pacific Palisades. Works that spring to mind include Phyllis Palmer's *Domesticity and*

XXI

Dirt: Housewives and Domestic Servants in the United States, 1920–1945, Evelyn Nakano Glenn's *Three Generations of Japanese American Women in Domestic Service*, and Judith Rollins's *Between Women: Domestics and Their Employers*.

Not to raise false hopes: the villa on San Remo Drive isn't mentioned in a single word in any of these books. And yet their findings can be compared with the conditions that prevailed there. The central conclusion of all these studies is broadly consistent with the daily routine at the Manns' residence. It reads as follows: The housewife of the middle and upper classes appears above all as the manager of her household. She compensates for her subordination to the status of her husband in the public sphere not only with her role as manager, but by also establishing her personal position of power through the hiring of servants from "lower" social classes, mostly people of color. This position of power and management is closely linked to a far-reaching division of organizational and physical work, to the extent that the housewife mostly just supervises the physically heavy or "menial" work (cleaning, laundry, etc.). Instead of carrying it out herself, she usually assigns it to personnel employed for this purpose.

The letters and diary entries of the individual Mann family members are ample proof that this form of the division of labor was cultivated on San Remo Drive as well, and that Katia Mann might serve as a role model for the type of household manager described by the American historians. Nevertheless, in Katia Mann's case, the sphere of the household went far beyond the actual house in terms of space and time. After all, she also took on the role of organizer of Thomas Mann's numerous journeys and long before the house on San Remo Drive could even be built had established the necessary groundwork for it to come into being. No wonder she was the one who discussed the plans with the architect Davidson, while Thomas Mann preferred to talk to him about his old hometown of Lübeck.

And yet as present as Katia Mann may have been under these circumstances, like the majority of middle- and upper-class housewives, she sacrificed her personal professional career to that of her husband and focused all her endeavors on the (wide) area of the household.

Here—between making, doing, and organizing—one could earn one's keep, which in the eyes of these women was the prerequisite for sharing in the status (and income) of their husbands. Seen in this light, Thomas Mann's work ethic found a perfect match in Katia Mann's work ethic, and it was left to her son Klaus to provide the appropriate description. "From nine o'clock in the morning until noon, magic was performed in the study. What Mother Mielein performed and achieved, not only from nine to twelve but all day long and every day anew, was likewise a kind of magic. Her duties are infinite; the sacrifices she must make innumerable. As she is only there for others, she hardly thinks of herself."

In other words, in American exile Katia Mann, who came from a wealthy Munich home, continued to earn her status with her work for the household, but also redefined her old role.

For Thomas Mann, the role of his wife was above all to be "guard and shelter" against the practical demands of the day and the unpleasantness of life. In that sense, Katia Mann was his female organizational expert.

She herself saw it the same way and put it thus: "Giving him a home was and remains my singular goal."

Not that women at the side or in the orbit of Thomas Mann could hope for much more than being female experts. Often and very quickly women would get on his nerves, no matter if they were patrons like Agnes Meyer, family members like the wife of his brother

Heinrich (whom he saw as a simpleton), or random "brainy biddies" who annoyed him.

Here Katia Mann held a special position, not only because she had married Thomas Mann and had six children and gone into exile with him, but also because she had created a familiar and comfortable environment for him on his travels and in foreign countries. It is therefore only too understandable that she had the Munich maids brought into exile in Switzerland and wanted to take the servants from Princeton with her to the house on San Remo Drive.

The fact that Katia Mann was always referred to in public as "Mrs. Thomas Mann "was, as it were, part of the history and idioms of the time — but her adoption of this name went so far that she had it printed on her own stationery and even referred to herself in this way long after Thomas Mann had passed away. But it did not stop there, because Mrs. Thomas Mann often became Mr. Thomas Mann during the lifetime of her husband, as it was always Katia who drafted letters in his name, wrote reviews of books he had not read, or negotiated contracts that he signed. This took time — and having time took servants.

How seriously Katia Mann took her role and how narrow the resulting structure of daily routines, social needs, and emotional sensitivities was for Thomas Mann (to live and to work) and his wife (to define her own position in the house as well as in the life of her husband) was most noticeable whenever Katia had to temporarily abandon the role of organizer and household manager and have someone else step in. In such situations, she would leave detailed instructions for those who were tasked with looking after her sensitive spouse: "Laying hen with rice, after gruel (made without stock) and perhaps a light dessert (lemon gratin, omelet soufflé or a light pudding), as a drink Fachinger mineral water," for example, were the orders to staff who accompanied Thomas Mann on a reading tour in 1932.

The fact that these tight arrangements—and instructions—were part of this special connection and thus independent of time and space is also illustrated by a letter that Katia Mann wrote eighteen years later during a trip to Chicago, to her husband, who had stayed at home. In it, she tells him that her daughter Erika should "buy soup meat for Saturday, beef-brisket, as lean as possible, approx. four pounds and six ounces, preferably at the Sunset Market beside the petrol stations."

On Sunday, however, Katia wrote further that it was better to go to the farmers market for the necessary errands, but this instruction was not, of course, to her husband, but to her daughter or one of the housekeepers, since while Thomas Mann knew the book market well he was oblivious to the farmers market.

Apart from the specifications for food acquisition, the letter also contains further directives, such as not to miss the forthcoming party hosted by the illustrator Eva Herrmann, who was a close friend of the family's and had made her house in Santa Barbara a central meeting place for the German émigré community.

In Thomas Mann's case, such reminders were not only well intentioned but also urgently needed. This is evidenced by the diary entries in which he repentantly declares that he had once again forgotten his wedding day. Since this lapse of memory happened not once but several times, over the years it developed into a small tradition in its own right, which had its advantages in spite of the bad conscience that the omission always induced: "The fact that the wedding day is forgotten does not necessarily have to be a bad sign, rather it attests to the consolidated implicitness of a marriage covenant."

Of course, things didn't go much better on his wife's birthdays, at least as far as presents were concerned, because Katia Mann usually bought them herself, draped them in the living room on the table, and organized the evening party—a small party, of course, not like the master's grand jubilee feasts where everyone who was anyone was invited.

Buying herself gifts was also practical, in that Katia Mann managed the family's finances anyway and, unlike her husband, knew well the family's income and expenses. And even though she had already played this role in Germany and in exile in Switzerland, she fit perfectly into the American way of life, because here, too, it was mostly women who acted as the financial directors of their households. For Katia Mann, however, keeping an overview was an absolute necessity, if only to give her writer husband the peace and quiet he needed.

Over their many years together this order of things was ingrained. Just how powerful it was (and how helpless it made Thomas Mann) can again be seen most clearly in those moments when external circumstances left a gap in the rhythm of the routines ... When Katia Mann was hospitalized in Zurich during a visit to Europe in 1950, Thomas Mann received a letter containing the biannual account for his books sold in America. According to his publisher, he was only entitled to nine dollars. To the author, who was spoiled by success and usually did not even get to see this kind of letter, such an insubstantial return was a shock—and a reason to keep the matter secret from his hospitalized wife, because he feared that the news would cause her great agitation and seriously undermine the healing process. When Thomas Mann came clean two days later and presented Katia with the paltry royalties, she was, to his surprise, highly amused. After all—as she immediately explained to her unsuspecting husband—the letter did not relate to sales in the United States, but rather to one of the typical additional payments from Canada. The American royalties, she assured him, would amount to the usual sum. A few thousand dollars, maybe even a dime or two more.

In other words, Katia Mann knew exactly what was going on even while she was in the hospital. And yet if one consults the aforementioned studies, they point to a factor that could easily be overlooked given this female financial administration. As much as women were the financial directors of their households, they were also expected — and expected of themselves — to spend money prudently. Not only because it was — at least in the majority of cases — money that had been earned by their husbands, but because in their own eyes prudence was a hallmark of good housekeeping. It was no different in "that amazing family." And "control" was indeed the operative term in the Mann household, not just in money matters ...

But there was more, and here too the individual case proves to be part of an established pattern. Because no matter how strong Katia Mann was, no matter how much she accomplished, knew, or decided for her husband, even in her case the traditional allocation of roles was not challenged. It was only "suspended" within the sphere of the household to the effect that the housewife retained authority over the employees and — by delegating tasks — had some degree of individual latitude. This, however, didn't lead to a reversal of the traditional order. From the outside — i.e., to all kinds of visitors — it might have seemed that Katia Mann was the gateway to Thomas Mann and that it was her who facilitated or to a degree even enabled his own access to public life outside the home. Yet she always remained "Mrs. Thomas Mann," the woman behind the great writer, the one who ran the household while he was writing and remained silent while he was speaking.

The fact that her managerial role involved a tremendous amount of work is all too obvious in view of the house on San Remo Drive and Thomas Mann's public role, as well as the large family and its sometimes quite peculiar members. Daughter Erika was of the opinion that her mother was slowly heading for canonization on account of what she had to endure "not only with the children and the gentle idiotic tyrannical uncle Heinrich, but also with the (countless) German petitioners, and what she does for all of them."

Well, the canonization was canceled, but the Protestant devotion to duty remained—and it was expected of the servants in equal measure. And yet in this respect, too, the housewife Katia Mann was only one of many, because almost all housewives in the upper and middle classes required the standards they set for themselves—in terms of performance, perseverance, and quality of work—from their staffs as well. As a result, expected workloads often led to overloads. And to misgivings—on all sides.

Countless letters from domestic workers, kept in the National Archives, bear witness to arduous working conditions—and also expose employers' lack of understanding. And even if no such testimonies are preserved from the employees of the Mann family, Thomas Mann's diaries and Katia Mann's letters do at least contain echoes of their voices. They give an impression of what it meant to be of service on San Remo Drive. A maid quit because her work was "too heavy"—a complaint that Thomas Mann could not comprehend, "because she had already been released from work in the upstairs rooms."

How many servants left San Remo Drive because of the working conditions there cannot be ascertained in retrospect, but their number was probably quite high considering the fact that most of them only stayed a few weeks, even a few days, and many left of their own accord.

But the other side also complained. Members of the Mann family repeatedly remarked that the staff did not live up to their accustomed standards nor the requirements of the house. Daughter Erika took the same line, but went one step further and blamed the (missing) domestic staff for her own unproductiveness: "For weeks, because of a complete lack of service (the yellow ones were first sick, then gone), absolutely nothing was accomplished. For the past few days, dark ones have been back in the house, but of little use."

In general, the work of the staff was rarely praised, and if so, it was mainly the male employees, such as the gardener Wataru, and their outwardly visible work that were remarked upon approvingly by the master or lady of the house. Thomas Mann's diaries contain little-to-no mention of any outstanding performance in the kitchen, while they are full of references to his displeasure with the food and service. He did, however, find ample words of praise whenever Katia herself stood in the kitchen, most likely because another cook had resigned.

But that's all too understandable. Thomas Mann knew exactly what he had in his wife—after all, it was Katia who always had his back, in Germany as well as in exile. And yet those who have someone else's back often stand with their own against the wall—and no one could express this better than their son Klaus, who stated in a letter that his mother's life played out in a "wide cul-de-sac."

Of course, Katia Mann's "cul-de-sac" might have been wider than that of most other housewives, and yet, in the end, she was only one of many women stuck in their homes. When Thomas Mann had been long dead, Katia Mann herself put her condition in a tragic nutshell: "I have never in my life been able to do what I would have wanted to do."

And she had wanted to do things and, under other circumstances, *in another life*, could have done them, too, because the housewives of the (American) middle and upper classes were often highly educated,

XXII

as Phyllis Palmer, in particular, points out repeatedly. Had Palmer known of Klaus Mann's letter, she would have found her own findings fully confirmed.

Klaus Mann wrote that his mother did not only speak excellent French and, unlike her husband, had learned to drive a car, but was also a master of "highest mathematics, Homer, all of Wagner's operas and all of Maupassant's short stories." Moreover, she had "furnished many villas, installed cooking pots," and "hated numerous cooks."

"Hate" is a word that conceals more than it reveals. Because Katia Mann's well-documented aversions to her domestic staff had a deeper source than mere personal animosity, even though this undoubtedly also played a role — and how could it be otherwise?

Yet the story does not end there, especially since those employees who might have been personally unpleasant for Katia Mann were hired by her in the first place, since she herself conducted all the interviews and determined who would and who wouldn't hold a position in the Mann household.

But the personnel problems at San Remo Drive were not only a question of the quality of the servants and the demands of the master and lady of the house, but also a question of quantity. After all, it was not easy to find domestic staff, especially during the war. This naturally strengthened the position of the employees, who were well aware of the general situation and the impending shortage in the house and tried to secure more rights, be it better (but still not good!) pay, shorter working hours (twelve hours was the rule), or various minor privileges.

So it's only understandable that during the war one held on to her domestic staff longer than usual, even if there were problems. A letter from Katia to Klaus Mann from the year 1943 is a case in point. "Since the beginning of the year," she writes, "we actually have a darkie again, by the name of Gussy, a very clever and reasonably hard-working thing. Only she keeps insisting on her days off from Wednesday to Friday and from Saturday to Monday, but at least for the rest of the time, she is a substantial relief for me. The fact that I had to give her my radio, of course, when there are no more to buy, hurts me."

The "darkie" is just one of many ethnic stereotypes found in the letters and diaries of the Mann family, which range from "the black" to "the yellow" to the "new Oscar" (representing the Mexicans). Countless documents confirm the fact that these stereotypes and the associated reductions were common in German émigré circles and constituted an integral part of "polite"— i. e., normal—speech. But they were also firmly anchored in American middle- and upper-class households—a fact pointed out by the historian David Katzman in 1978 when he published his study *Seven Days a Week: Women and Domestic Service in Industrializing America*. He found that the reduction to stereotypes represented an essential operational resource by which the household could be sustained on the inside and presented as a functioning enterprise to the outside. The devaluation of people of color as second-class and the treatment of domestic staff as lower-level workers went hand in hand.

But there was another factor that is illuminated again and again in multiple studies and contemporary sources: in the eyes of the (American) middle and upper classes, people of color were regarded as a group in need of leadership, as people who were unable to control their own lives without supervision—a role that was assumed by the (white) housewives.

The Manns' dismissal of a German Jewish couple with an "ignorant semi-education" and subsequent return to representatives of the "friendly Negro tribe," who were often less educated due to their social background, was thus understandable—an act of differentiation in which one could enlarge oneself and at the same time assume leadership from that elevated position.

The fact that this claim to leadership was reinforced and apparently legitimized by errant behavior, as in the case of Felix and Joe, only made the whole thing appear more natural.

In other words, not only was one (including Mann) allowed to be served, it was essentially one's duty to be served. And what could be nicer than a champagne dinner with friends in a grand house, "with three black waiters by the light of grandmother's candelabras"?

Besides, this differentiation—the construction of black domestic workers as "others"—helped the white housewife to perceive herself as a subject rather than an object of the household. Although she essentially worked in the house just like the servants, she merely assigned the chores, especially the laborious ones, to others, and consequently represented the head of the whole enterprise.

But another facet becomes clear when seen in the light of the studies mentioned earlier: many of the women of color who took on jobs as "maids" or "domestic servants" were relatively young and often unmarried, which was due to their long working hours, low incomes, and sometimes being required to live where they worked. Thus, in addition to ethnic and social differences, an age gap could also be effectively constructed, in the sense that the young servants would need to be educated by the lady of the house ("the mother")—a role that Katia Mann knew how to fill perfectly. And in the end, it didn't matter if the female servants were already thirty or forty years old, since Katia Mann's own daughters were no younger. For her, servants were always "girls" who had to be educated.

The idea of supervision, education, and leadership associated with the black servants was, of course, difficult to associate with German-émigré domestic-service couples, which was one reason why the Macha and Hahn couples each stayed only two weeks.

With Felix and Joe, things were very different. With them, the belief in the possibility of being able to educate the representatives of the "friendly Negro tribe"—indeed the perceived duty to do so—led the Manns to rehire them and to take their renewed misconduct not as a reason for immediate dismissal, but as a cause for social measures within the household. This went on until in the view of the Mann family the servants had proved to be completely resistant to learning.

But black servants like Felix and Joe are not the only ones who were "rewarded" with this specific form of charity. A reflection of the same attitude can be found in one of Thomas Mann's letters, which says of Koto and Wataru: "They had become acquainted with the agonies of humiliation in the camp and tried to restore themselves economically by serving."

Service as a way of building a new life for oneself—another example of the diffuse triad of patronizing charity, social intervention, and exercise of power which seems to have shaped the way staff was treated in the Mann household. That it could establish itself in this way was at least partially because Japanese Americans were often only allowed to leave the internment camps if they had proof or at least the prospect of employment. Thus it was bureaucratic as well as economic circumstances—Koto had earned hardly anything in the camp—that compelled them to accept any job they could get. Several agencies were established in the LA area after 1942 to act as intermediaries in the placement of former camp inmates.

However—and here too the testimonies from San Remo Drive

correspond to the results of numerous studies—Japanese Americans were viewed differently from African Americans. While the latter, in the eyes of the master and lady of the house, required leadership to steer their lives in the "right" direction, Japanese Americans were regarded primarily as Japanese who were considered to be naturally calm and submissive, which—in the final step of this construction—led to them being seen as the perfect servants.

When Thomas Mann spoke of Koto and Wataru, it was probably no coincidence that they were "the best servants we have ever had, civilized, well behaved, diligent, clean. And they bow so neatly, their flat hands on their thighs."

And yet this polarized characterization is complemented by a commonality attributed to African and Japanese Americans alike: that it was their destiny to serve—whether by nature or because their social backgrounds did not allow them to live otherwise.

And only when they proved to be completely incapable of learning or were simply too old—so that that the mode of education could no longer be effective or any help was "naturally" futile—were they dismissed. "Old Negroes," "all too clumsy," was the comment concerning a service couple in 1947, while Thomas Mann had written to his patron Agnes Meyer in January 1942, a few days before moving into the villa on San Remo Drive, explaining to her the departure of the previous servant John: "He had been feeble and not much use for a while."

Such stereotyping and its reduction to origin, skin color, and utility (as well as their associated hierarchies) were also reflected in the fact that where there were servants from different ethnic groups—as was the case in the Mann household—further differentiations were made.

During the often months-long travels of the Mann family, the villa on San Remo Drive was not taken care of by the black domestic workers, since they could neither be supervised nor educated in any way from a distance. Instead, Koto or Wataru were brought back for a few weeks, or someone from the surrounding émigré community was asked to water the flowers and receive the mail while the family was away, which is why sometimes on San Remo Drive, German philosophers could be observed tending to the garden and pacifist poets could be seen struggling with mountains of paper.

Felix and Joe, on the other hand, were passed over, and when the Manns travelled to Europe for a few months in May 1949, Katia made it clear to them six weeks in advance that friends of her daughter Erika's would be taking care of the villa, whereupon Felix and Joe "vacated the house, leaving behind the greatest disorder and taking the silver coffee pot with them." What remained was a property liberated once again from domestic staff—and the newly consolidated insight that this "ungrateful rabble" was unable to deal with the hardships of life and in desperate need of control and guidance.

In addition to these diffuse and often subliminal motives, there was another very practical reason that prompted Katia and Thomas Mann to choose mostly black servants, even though they sometimes meant additional trouble and upset. In contrast to the German émigrés who also applied for positions in the San Remo Drive residence, black servants only understood and spoke English, which Thomas Mann certainly appreciated. When "hardly a word of English was spoken in the house" due to the construction work and the German domestic-service couple that had first been hired, he complained bitterly about it and longed for the return of his black servants. The fact that they did not understand German also had the advantage that no private matters could escape the house—a problem which, especially in the vicinity of Hollywood, affected quite a few households where gossip would all too often reach the salons, church congregations, or simply the neighborhoods.

From this perspective, the preferred recruitment of black servants in the Mann household was not primarily motivated by economics. The decisive factors were social and cultural and included traditional notions of work and ethnic stereotypes. Also, people of color were accustomed to long working hours due to their socialization and professional experience, and had no trade-union representation. This was compounded by a lack of regulation of working hours and wages, and finally by the fact that people of color were excluded from many professions in America until the 1950s, which further increased their concentration (and the wage pressure on them) in domestic employment. Only once were questions of payment disputed in the San Remo Drive residence. And it is no coincidence that this conflict occurred in August 1942, at a time when America was in its first year of war and the arms industry was booming throughout the country.

In August 1942, a black domestic-service couple left the family, enticed, as Thomas Mann wrote, "by a naturally much higher-paid defense job for the husband. So they can start their own home, have a baby and all that—perfectly understandable from their point of view, but we are stranded because replacement is hard to come by." And then, as if to draw a conclusion: "The servant problem has always been difficult in America, and the war makes a solution almost impossible unless you can offer huge wages."

The statement sums up much of what has already been described: young, still-childless people of color as servants, the advantages in the choice of jobs offered to them by the war, their departures to establish themselves independently, the problems of the family in finding new staff, and the belief that one could earn "huge wages" in this business—a misconception, given that even during the war monthly wages amounted to less than $50 for a twelve-hour work day, six days a week.

On the other hand, there was the praise of the work of one's own family, because once the servants were gone, it was Erika who "bravely cooks." But she too soon left, and all that remained was the hope that "there may be some being who is no good for anything else and who can provide for us." Servitude as a last resort — for the servants as well as for the master.

But the hierarchies were still expressed on another, downright inconspicuous level, namely in the names given — or not given — to the servants. In their studies on this subject, the sociologists Judith Rollins and Mary Romero have provided valuable insights that I would never have come across by myself.

According to Rollins and Romero, the masters and their wives often addressed the black servants by their first names only. You could also say they spoke to them like children.

At San Remo Drive the servants were summoned in the same way, and their reduction to first names is perpetuated to this day through Mann's published diaries and letters. And to someone like Thomas Mann, who knew how to express his distance to God and the world better than anyone else, this focus on first names is unusual. This is illustrated by the fact that it took him thirty-four years until he started to address his best friend, the conductor Bruno Walter, who also lived in exile in California, with the informal German pronoun "Du."

The fact that Thomas Mann would call his employees by their first names from day one can therefore only be explained by the power dynamic, which justified derogation in all directions. Because one

XXIII

thing is certain: in Thomas Mann's diaries, Katia Mann's letters, and in the documents received from Klaus and Erika Mann, the African, Mexican, and Japanese Americans working on San Remo Drive were almost without exception mentioned by their first names only, insofar as they didn't appear under stereotypical epithets such as "the yellows," "the blacks," or so on for other colors, races, ethnic groups, or tribes.

The émigré couple Macha, on the other hand, appeared under their surname only. The German Jewish couple Hahn was only known by their surname as well. This time there were no first names, and only once was there a hint at possible choices in naming.

When Thomas Mann wrote a letter to his former private secretary in Princeton, Hans Meisel, on February 1, 1942, to announce that a German Jewish married couple named Hahn would soon be joining him, his usual flow of words suddenly stalled, and Thomas Mann asked himself (and his former secretary) whether he ought to address the future servant as "Herr Hahn."

Two small worlds collided, and in the process, the limits of what could be said as well as the power of habit were revealed. Until now Thomas Mann had always called his (colored) servants by their first names, but now German Jews were coming to the house—and the question of salutation posed a problem. Thomas Mann resolved it in his own way: social proximity precipitated salutatory separation, and in the end only the "Hahn couple" remained, a man and a woman whose first names were never mentioned and haven't yet been determined.

Viewed in this way, the names were indeed signs. That Thomas Mann didn't refer to men like Ted Löwenstein, Julius Ralph Davidson, Ernst Schlesinger, or Paul Huldschinsky as "Ted", "Ralph", "Ernst", or "Paul" in his notes may seem natural to the reading eye. But there was a compelling reason for it. They did not function as representatives of any more or less friendly "tribe," and what appears as natural order turns out to be a historical construct.

And yet, to say it as clearly as possible, especially in times like these, when the cult of purification celebrated by those whose speech is oh so clean and correct and whose perception is purged of history: it has by no means been the intent of this chapter to condemn the stereotypes used by Thomas or Katia Mann, to criticize the language of their letters and diaries or to shout "racism!" This would be an injustice both to the Mann family and to history as a whole, and would imply intent where speech was determined by contemporary patterns rather than retrospective insights. The historicity of history must be preserved at all times and it is not the duty of literature to speak "correctly," even where it undertakes a brief excursion into the world of academe. On the contrary, if literature has any duty at all, it consists in emphasizing the historicity of all life and recognizing that to think historically, in the dual sense of the word, means to be indulgent. Language remains messy, until the very end.

And now, as promised, let's talk about the weather ...

The Weather Back Then
or
How the Climate Is Changing

The year 1949 begins with a loss as the area around Pacific Palisades loses its reputation as a frost-free region. Instead, there are subfreezing temperatures for days on end, snow, and arctic winds. California, it seems, is becoming an ice palace.

Due to the low temperatures, an electric heater has to be installed in the hallway of the villa on San Remo Drive, but soon the fuses are blown, the power supply is interrupted, the house is cold, and Thomas Mann is annoyed. It takes the electrician almost two weeks to fix the problem. As soon as he's gone and the thaw has set in, a few canal workers arrive on San Remo Drive and start tearing up the road in front of the house.

"Exit almost impossible. Plus noise," the diary reports. It is no wonder that Thomas Mann sits in his study with an earache. Outside, the family Buick rolls backward down the driveway as a result of a handbrake not being applied, and only with some effort and the help of the construction workers can the car be brought to a standstill.

Meanwhile, Thomas Mann sits tired on his sofa and learns by telephone that his brother Viktor, who remained in Germany during the war, has died unexpectedly at the age of fifty-nine. Three days later Thomas Mann leaves for his old homeland.

The journey has been planned for a long time. It is supposed to bring Thomas Mann, his wife Katia, and daughter Erika back to Germany via Great Britain, Sweden, Switzerland, and the Netherlands, but the homecoming does not go as planned. In Stockholm, Thomas Mann learns that his son Klaus has killed himself. An overdose of sleeping pills has brought an end to a life fraught with turnarounds. Klaus Mann dies on May 21, 1949, in Cannes, France. It's a lonely death. When he is buried on May 24, his brother Michael is the only family member by his graveside. And even that is a coincidence because Michael Mann is only at the funeral because Cannes is a stop on the European tour of the orchestra in which he is playing. He makes it just in time for the interment. As he stands in front of the open grave, he takes out his viola and plays one last serenade for his brother who lies six feet below him in a wooden box. He couldn't know that Klaus had imagined the final act to be quite different ... "If anything should happen to me, I want to be cremated without any ceremony — no speeches, please! no music! no flowers."

A short time later, there are speeches, music, and flowers for Thomas Mann as well, but in his case, the occasion is not a funeral but a birthday. Johann Wolfgang von Goethe will be two hundred years old, and it is this anniversary that has led Thomas Mann to leave San Remo Drive and return to Germany for the first time after sixteen years in exile, because he has been promised the prestigious Goethe Prize there. There are, in fact, two Goethe Prizes, since Germany is by now divided and each side believes it is on the right side of history. Thomas Mann first receives the West German Goethe Prize in Frankfurt, and a few days later the East German Goethe National Prize in Weimar.

At this time, at the end of July 1949, he has already blocked out the suicide of his son Klaus, burying him under presentations and prizes. Georges Motschan, who has known Thomas and Katia Mann for years, chauffeurs them through Germany in his car for weeks and never leaves their side during their journey. He is surprised to find that Klaus is not spoken about in public, and that even in private conversations "the name of the deceased is never mentioned."

Displacement, self-control, and a certain severity against oneself and others are three of the coins Thomas and Katia Mann use to pay for a life that befits their social standing. Their son Klaus, on the other hand, gave up his own for a different existence.

Shortly thereafter, on August 19, 1949, Thomas and Katia Mann return to Pacific Palisades, where Thomas Mann finds "fruits and flowers" in the rooms instead of the usual mountains of paper, and even with the poodle things seem to have gone better than last time — at least he hasn't run away, but only scratched the carpet in the study, while his master was out of the country.

Not to worry. Thomas Mann is happy to be home again; he feels safe in his study and enjoys the comforts of his Californian home. At least until the power goes out again, the fuses are blown, and it again grows dark and cold in the house.

Because he understands the problem, this time the electrician can sort it out within two hours. When he's gone, the sun is shining outside and everything's fine. San Remo is empty. No one tears open the road, and no one dumps a stack of sewer pipes in front of the family's house. Yet Thomas Mann still suffers from earaches and feels his peace and quiet disturbed. This is because after October the villa will become a hangout for local handymen.

A new bookshelf will be installed in the passage to the study, the hot-water boiler in the boiler room will be repaired, the living room will have freshly upholstered armchairs, and the house's five bathrooms will be retiled.

It looks as if the Mann family doesn't want to leave California anymore, and only a dead lemon tree has to go — it is removed from the garden and taken home as firewood by the Mexican workers.

Three days after the tree has been torn out of the ground, rats show up and begin to infest the property as well as the house.

"A plague of rats," says the diary on December 8. And then: "Tonight in the studio they got the big tin box with chocolate from the bookshelf, knew how to open it and ate almost all the contents."

There isn't much the hastily summoned pied piper can do, though, and when he finds one of the greedy rodents and kills it with a shovel, the real problem is not solved either, because just as invasive rats pilfer the food in the house, a thought begins to gnaw at Thomas Mann's mind.

"Discussion of our resettlement to Switzerland," he notes in his diary on December 21, 1949, and then: "Commotion of life."

This is the beginning of the end. And even though it will still take two and a half years until the final departure, doubts against the move will continue to stack up on the pages of the diary; from now on every step back is only made for the purpose of taking a run-up. And that is necessary. It is a big task, after all, to leave a whole country behind, to cross the Big Pond, to make the jump. To exit from exile.

The reasons for Thomas Mann's drawn-out departure from America are as numerous as they are varied. They range from the political changes in the country and his fear that a new fascism might emerge in America, to the public attacks against him because of his antifascist attitude, which after the war is interpreted by some hecklers as sympathy for the Communists. This is aggravated by his visit to the Goethe event in Weimar, where the Russians rule, and the problems of his daughter Erika, who has been denied American citizenship and who pushes for a break with the country, just like her brother Golo, who works as a college teacher but likes "neither the country, nor the countryside, nor politics, nor teaching," and considers America to be "increasingly hysterical, unfriendly, and gloomy." In addition, the family is being watched by the FBI—and as the number of surveillance records goes up, the number of lectures, awards, and honorariums goes down ... In short, "All hopes once pinned on this country are completely disappointed."

And Europe? Now that the days in America are growing darker, it regains some of its old splendor. Thomas Mann wants to be buried in his homeland; he has the feeling that he can only truly be at home in Europe. This wish is nourished by an ever-dwindling circle of friends in America as many acquaintances return to the Old World.

It's as if someone has turned over the great hourglass of fate a second time and flipped it from the Californian head onto its former feet again—and now everyone is trickling back to where they had come from. The strange country served as their home for a time, and there were even moments when they felt that "emigration" was indeed an anagram for "Ort in Magie" (German for "place of magic"). But now the spell is broken.

It is no wonder that even the one his family simply calls "the magician" thinks about leaving. There are plenty of reasons—that much is clear. There are good reasons, big reasons, provable reasons. Reasons that can be found in letters, diaries, and footnotes. And yet the story of a single individual never tallies with the big picture. In other words, if you are looking for reasons to move, you must also read the weather report. And you mustn't forget the rats that come and steal the chocolate from the bookshelf. Who knows if they might not go for the books next? And in any case, are accidents and catastrophes in America not generally on the rise? And why is San Remo Drive getting darker and wetter? Why do the gas heaters go out and why is the power supply permanently interrupted?

It's as if it were these small, inconspicuous reasons — the capricious weather, the calamities of the house, and the small catastrophes around the place — that prompt Thomas Mann to think about his return in the first place. And once the thought is there, it will find reasons. Good reasons. Big reasons. Further reasons. Reasons that reach as far as Europe. Reasons that do not even take note of the 1949 weather forecast or interpret it entirely as historical happenstance. In the days before the idea of resettlement arises, the much-praised Californian climate dons an apocalyptic pinafore …

12.18.1949: "Rain, all night long. Continues."
12.19.1949: "The rain, which had paused during the night, sets in again."
12.20.1949: "Very cold wind."

On December 21: thoughts of resettlement, the commotion of life, the desire to find tranquility in the old homeland.
Meanwhile, in California, the wind drives new rain against the house. "Eerie conditions" prevail. "Fog cloud" and "fog darkness" alternate and finally turn into misery on January 8: "Rain and darkness all day long. In the afternoon a longer interruption of the electrical current. Cold and darkness. Slept through the bad time."

Then, at the end of the month, the awakening:
01.30.1950: "It's getting serious. Feeling of general crisis and a turning point."

But doubts remain, and who knows whether there is a way back at all?

01.31.1950: "Horror and nausea. I can't cope with the conditions in this country, but I can't countenance the thought of abandoning the house."

XXIV

02.01.1950: "How close is death!"

Today, in the year 2018, it is easy to answer this rhetorical question, because today I know that after February 1, 1950, Thomas Mann has exactly 2,018 days to live. But there is one who is no longer among the living at that point, because Niko, the poodle, is dead.

At least he hasn't returned from his last amorous adventure, and all efforts to find him are in vain.

"His danger was and always has been the female," Thomas Mann writes to a friend, and his only consolation is that the animal was already old and he won't have to watch it die, because that would be even worse for him than watching a human die … "age is showing in the fact that love seems to have drained from me and it is a long time since I have seen a human face for which I could mourn. My mind is only amiably moved by the sight of a creature, of beautiful dogs, poodles, and setters."

Young Swiss waiters, Argentine tennis players, and various boys on the beach of Santa Monica also move — not to say, excite — Thomas Mann's mind. But that is always just temptation, never fulfillment — and in this respect, Niko was different …

He was eternally tempted by the female — and eternally gave in to temptation. And even when he was home, he still had a sweet tooth. "Just recently, behind our backs, he had taken a whole cupcake from the table and eaten it," Thomas Mann told his friend Alfred Neumann on January 13, 1950, not without a certain pride. But Niko has been missing for almost two weeks now.

"The end of an eleven-year cohabitation," Thomas Mann notes in his diary.

Eleven years—that's the complete duration of his American exile.

A new poodle will soon be brought into the house by air freight from Philadelphia, but that's no real consolation.

It is basically the same with the animal as with the land, on the small and large scale—the new is not the old. Another poodle, another America. It doesn't even help to name the dog after Alger Hiss, the high-ranking employee of the American State Department whom McCarthy's commie hunters had sentenced and imprisoned a few days earlier for alleged Russian espionage.

Like Alger Hiss, Algi the dog is handed over to a taskmaster, because he wets all the carpets in the house. His reeducation is to last six weeks. For the time being, life goes on without him on San Remo Drive, even though it's sad: pee-stained carpets inside, shitty weather outside. Lots of rain, no sun. "Always grey and dark."

In California, the Cold War culminates in a small climatic catastrophe, and even when the rain abates for a while and Thomas Mann can go out and take his usual walks, nothing is as it used to be. The California Riviera has changed its face completely. There's construction everywhere.

Up the road: "New buildings."
Down the road: "New buildings."
View from above over the village: "Many new buildings."

The result: a feeling of alienation, oppression, melancholy. Suffering, fear, and anguish alternate, and bring this: "Thoughts of escape, again and again."

Shortly afterward, on March 11, 1950, Thomas Mann's brother Heinrich dies. They lived close to each other for ten years, but they were never really close.

Heinrich Mann had not found his place in America. After his wife's suicide in December 1944, he had lived with his brother's family in the house on San Remo Drive for a while and later, in September 1947, he had moved back into the villa for a few days after his doctor recommended that he do just that to overcome his depression. So he sat at the table in the evening, smiled, seemed apathetic, didn't listen, and talked, if at all, about his own problems, which led to the other members of the family soon becoming depressed as well.

Fortunately, Katia rented a small apartment for him in Santa Monica, and Heinrich Mann finally moved in there. There he was, in a blue silk robe, sitting between countless books and pictures, living off his memories. And in spite of that, he continued to write, day after day, often ten hours or more, and during this time was not available for anyone, regardless of whoever rang the bell. Even when he went out, he remained alone, looking "bewildered by the hustle and bustle of people: averse, closed to their language, their mentality," a stranger in a strange land, one who wasted away with time and finally one night ceased living.

What follows are big routines and little discoveries. Katia organizes the transfer of the body. Thomas discusses the ceremony with the pastor. Erika discovers drawings of fat, naked women in Heinrich's apartment. Golo picks them up to destroy them in order to protect the memory of his uncle.

Once that's done, there are wreaths, flowers, and classical music. This is followed by the usual speeches.

When the family leaves the cemetery, the coffin in which Heinrich Mann lies is still laid out on the lawn. Not even in death, it seems, has he found his place in America.

Thomas Mann, on the other hand, is becoming more and more obsessed with his thoughts of escape. A journey should bring distraction and give him a feeling of freedom.

In May 1950, Thomas, Katia, and Erika Mann return to Europe once again. This time the destination is Switzerland, but the Manns soon have to leave their hotel and look for another one—a plague of rats in one of their rooms forces them out. Their new homeland seems to catch up with them even in the Old World. And there's a lot going on besides.

Thomas Mann loses his heart to a waiter.
Katia Mann loses weight after cosmetic surgery.
Erika Mann loses her desire to return to America.

But by the end of August, regardless, the family is back again. In Pacific Palisades. In America. In "gangster land."

Instead of fruits and flowers, it's piles of paper again this time—and Algi, the poodle, is also back from the dog trainer. Instead of chasing the ladies, however, he prefers to chase after the lemons Thomas Mann throws to him in the garden. It is probably the most athletic activity of a man who has so little interest in sports that he manages to write hundreds of letters and fill thousands of diary pages in fourteen years of exile in America without even once mentioning the words "football," "basketball," or "baseball," let alone speak of attending any actual sporting events. The enthusiasm for sports and the great role that it plays in the everyday lives of Americans remain so incomprehensible to Thomas Mann that they aren't even a mystery to him, but only feature as a blank space in his American years.

What else? Thomas Mann continues to be troubled by the country and perceives an increasing threat in the situation. The Red Scare seems to drive all of America to distraction. Even the dog is going crazy. His six weeks of reeducation were obviously a waste of time.

10. 26. 1950: "The poodle piddling psychopathically."
11. 13. 1950: "Calamity with the wet and dirty poodle."
01. 01. 1951: "Walked alone with the poodle who jumped into a swimming pool and had to be rescued."

Thomas Mann considers giving the dog to Krishnamurti since it would probably take an Indian scholar with a peace of mind as large as all of California to come to grips with it. But the poodle gets wind of the matter, sneaks into Thomas Mann's study one fine Sunday, nestles up to him, and involves the writer in a "prolonged sorrowful dialogue."

The result: the dog stays, Thomas Mann continues to toss lemons into the garden, and Krishnamurti flies back to India on his own in the autumn of 1951.

But, of course, this doesn't solve the problems, especially since now that the poodle is finally behaving, the house is beginning to act up. Sometimes the heater emits a burning smell, sometimes it is defective, and sometimes it just blows cold air into the rooms. That wouldn't be too bad, of course, if some doors didn't start jamming while others stopped closing properly. Soon the thrill of impending departure is dimmed by a chill of insufferable drafts. And what's worse is that everyone can watch the family as they all shiver and quiver, because one by one even the Venetian blinds fail and are dismantled and taken away for repair.

Outside of the house, things aren't much better. The bad weather has severely affected the garden, and Thomas Mann's bedroom balcony is also in bad shape. Leaves have clogged the drain for weeks, until even Thomas Mann, who hardly ever sets foot on his balcony, can no longer overlook the matter, although it isn't the small pool that has formed there which attracts his attention, but rather the damp patches that begin to grace the ceiling of his study one floor below.

In other words, the whole house is in urgent need of renovation, but the costs are quite high, and even if things were different the question would still arise of whether the renovations were worth it, because to Thomas Mann the house seems too big and too expensive for his family, which has by now shrunk to three people.

The compromise between beauty and size, on the one hand, and decay and cost, on the other, is made as follows: the house will get a nice facelift, not for the sake of the family's own quality of life but so that they may rent it out.

And because this requires some money, in May 1951 the neighboring property is sold. The Manns had acquired it in March 1945; it is not clear from the family's records what this property was, nor why it was purchased then.

Was it because the master of the house wanted to have his peace and could not bear more annoying neighbors? Or was it an object of speculation, a piece of land that had been bought to be resold at a profit, and that in the meantime had functioned as an in-house lemon plantation, even if it wasn't the Manns who brought in the harvest, but rather a few Mexicans?

To be honest, I don't know. There simply aren't any documents. After leafing through the pages of the LA land register, however, it is at least possible to name the piece of land that was sold in May 1951. It was just over half an acre directly behind Thomas Mann's house, and it officially belonged to 1560 San Remo Drive—one of the few lots that were still undeveloped at that time.

The price Thomas Mann gets for this property is $10,200.

Then it's on to Europe, where the family will spend the summer. The departure will take place on the Fourth of July, to coincide with American Independence Day.

While Thomas Mann is still crossing the Atlantic, his former neighbor Arnold Schönberg passes away in Los Angeles. The two had not had much to say to each other in recent years, after Thomas Mann had used Schönberg's twelve-tone technique for his novel *Doctor Faustus* but hadn't credited Schönberg sufficiently in the latter's eyes. Reason enough for Schönberg to terminate his friendship with the writer and publicly accuse him of stealing intellectual property.

Thomas Mann had tried to settle the debate just as publicly in December 1948 by telling Schönberg that he should "rise above bitterness and mistrust and find peace in the certain consciousness of his greatness and fame."

Two and a half years later, on July 13, 1951, Arnold Schönberg finds his peace in death. He, who was born on a thirteenth and had developed an almost insane fear of this number in the course of his life, was certain that he would die on a thirteenth—and that this thirteenth could only be a Friday.

And that's indeed how it happened. On Friday, July 13, 1951, Arnold Schönberg barricaded himself in the living room of his house on North Rockingham Avenue, sitting in his armchair staring at the hands of the clock and hoping that the day would simply pass. After the clock had finally struck midnight, Schönberg was relieved and went up to his bedroom. When his wife wanted to bring him a night-cap a little later, she found her husband lying motionless on the floor. He'd fallen over, right in front of the bedroom clock.

The reason was as simple as it was deadly: this clock had not yet struck twelve and the thirteenth was still in full swing. That the fright-ening day had already been rung out by the living-room clock was due to the fact that that clock had been fast for many years, by a full quarter of an hour. Now it was too late to set the clock back.

Arnold Schönberg died on Friday, July 13, 1951, thirteen minutes before midnight, at the age of seventy-six — a figure whose digit sum also equals thirteen.

And Thomas Mann? He can at least console himself with the fact that Schönberg had made him a peace offering in one of his last letters. "Let's bury the hatchet," he had written, but immediately pointed out that he would not make the reconciliation public until a few years later, when he was eighty, so as not to annoy those who had taken his side in the *Faustus* affair. Now it wasn't going to happen at all.

In October, the Mann family returns to America from their trip to Europe — and their arrival day befits their status. "California. Blue sky," Thomas Mann notes in his diary. And: "The house as pleasant as ever."

A little later he gets a visitor. "A semi-fledged little sparrow who can't even get over the balustrade" sits on his balcony and doesn't know what to do. He can't go up to heaven, and he won't go down to earth, for there the dog makes his rounds, and everyone knows that he who hunts lemons also bites sparrows.

But maybe Thomas Mann remembered the anecdote for a completely different reason and only wrote it down because he is just as fledgling as the sparrow. And it doesn't matter that he's already seventy-six years old now. The problem is that he's stuck, just like the sparrow. Between the blue Californian sky, under which he can breathe so well, and the European earth, where he wants to be buried.

Five weeks later the scales have tilted, and the pendulum of fate points eastward. "Departure highly advisable," the diary says on November 22. And to stop his head from overturning this decision again, the alternatives are also listed. War, the lynching frenzy, and a terrible depression — that's what awaits the Manns if they stay in America.

To finally break away from America and also to have money for a reasonable retirement in Europe, the family has to sell the house on San Remo Drive. However, the question arises: How much is this place actually worth?

$35,000 — that's all they will get, Thomas Mann says, but he is laughed at by everyone for this estimate. $70,000, says Davidson, the architect who comes by for tea with his wife, but Mann should start with $90,000. $90,000 is a bit much, so Thomas Mann asks $75,000 and finds a real-estate agent who can hardly wait to get the green light to sell the house.

But $75,000 is too much given the house's structural condition, another agent is sure — $70,000 is the upper limit.

As always, speculators have the last word.

But before it is time, the Californian earth spirits crash the party. Not to show Thomas Mann what he misses when he's gone, but to confirm to him that it's a damn good idea not to be buried here.

12.25.1951: "Around 1:25 a. m. Earthquake with tremors of the bed, cracking and sounding. No rest."

12.29.1951: "It continues to rain. Ceiling damage from roof dripping onto the balcony from above."

12.30.1951: "Infinite rain. Lots of water damage. Eucalyptus uprooted in the garden."

01.18.1952: "Interruption of the rain. The number of those killed has risen to six. Schools closed today. Many roads closed. Many evacuations, where the mud penetrated the houses."

And then, on January 23: "Yesterday 'exclusive' contract signed with the estate agent."

Shortly thereafter, the usual yard sign is put up by the roadside, while upstairs in the house the carpets, furniture, and windows are cleaned one last time and Thomas Mann receives calls about his "break with America."

There are no buyers yet, however, even when the villa on San Remo Drive is advertised in the *Los Angeles Times* for the first time on January 27 and the agent has the temerity to praise the house as a "Famed Author's Home." No wonder that some of the prospective buyers who have the villa shown to them only come to see which famous author lives there. Thomas Mann is soon annoyed by the impertinent rabble taking tours of his house out of pure curiosity — as if it were a museum and he its prize exhibit.

But who knows, maybe he is just that, but he's only noticed it now. Perhaps he only now realizes that the German enclave in California can no longer be held because America's philistinism is wafting through the door. And this isn't only due to the weather ("Infinite rain, at times excessive. The Sunset a torrent"), but also to the fact that hordes of happy people enter his living room. Because that's exactly what happens.

On June 21, three days before the departure, to everyone's surprise, the real-estate agent appears at San Remo Drive. He hadn't been here for a while, and it looked as if the house might be impossible to sell. But now things have changed—and fundamentally. At any rate, the agent is standing on the terrace, grinning from ear to ear, with dollar signs in his eyes. And he has every reason for this because behind him there is not only a potential buyer but a whole group of interested parties. Thomas Mann is scared stiff and after the agent has said a few words he can only watch how the people push one by one into his house.

He had originally planned, after no buyer had been found, for his nephew Klaus Pringsheim to live here. Just the day before, this nephew had come from New York and moved into one of the guest rooms so as to make all the necessary arrangements and, as soon as the Mann family finds a new home in Europe, to organize the shipment of their furniture. But now these American buyers are crawling all over the house—and the furniture is the last thing that interests them. If one of them should decide to buy the house, the Manns will only have four weeks to vacate the villa, pack everything, and send it back to Switzerland.

It won't come to that, though. In the end, nobody wants the house, and maybe it's not only because of the price but also the light yellowish hue the painters recently applied to all exterior walls. The work was intended to freshen up the house, but the color has created the opposite impression, and now that the house is to be sold, it looks as if the whole family has been chain-smoking on the terrace for years.

It is June 21, 1952. Exactly eleven years ago, Thomas Mann signed a contract with Ernst Schlesinger for the construction of the house. In Europe at that time, the architecture of the world was on the brink of collapse. Now it is on the brink again — the only difference being, according to Thomas Mann, that the future conflicts will take place in America. It seems as if the fog of darkness has supplanted enlightenment.

"Farewell," Thomas Mann notes in his diary the next morning. And then it's over.

On June 24, 1952, Thomas and Katia Mann leave Pacific Palisades. Five days later, they board a plane in New York that takes them to Zurich via Amsterdam. This time, this much is certain: there will be no return.

In Switzerland, Even Downward Spirals
Wind Up at Tolerable Heights

In Switzerland, Thomas and Katia Mann first rent a house in Erlenbach, a community on Lake Zurich, just a few hundred yards from Küsnacht, where they lived between 1933 and 1938. The area is called the "Goldcoast" because of its opulent residences and their wealthy inhabitants.

Some six thousand miles away, not far from the US Pacific Coast, their old house is still empty. So far no buyer has been found. The property is not being well maintained since the nephew who is supposed to take care of the house is only present occasionally, and when Thomas Mann's son Golo arrives in August, he is shocked by the "beautiful, melancholically dilapidated house."

Some of the household goods have already been collected and some have been packed into boxes, while the library has also shrunk because the books Thomas Mann considers important have long been moved to Switzerland. But about three and a half thousand books are still there, and soon Klaus Pringsheim receives the order from Katia Mann to sell them.

He goes to a bookseller in Santa Monica and explains the situation.

"I have Thomas Mann's private library, thousands of books, would you like to buy them?"
"Yes," says the bookseller.
"What would you pay for it?" the nephew asks.
"Five cents for a book."
"For God's sake, this is the library of a Nobel laureate! And the personal library of Thomas Mann! You have to give more!"
"No, it doesn't say in the books that they belonged to Thomas Mann."

That's the end of that conversation — the entire library is thus worth less than $200.
But the books are sold anyway because they must leave the house.

Because there are so many of them, the bookseller doesn't just bring a few helpers, but also a truck. Because the books are so heavy, the helpers use a shovel to dump them onto the truck's bed. The thermometer shows ninety-five degrees Fahrenheit and they work up quite a sweat.

Meanwhile, Golo Mann is asked by his parents living in Switzerland to send them their winter clothes.

Klaus Pringsheim begins to arrange the remains of Thomas Mann's record collection. Thomas Mann took his favorite records with him when he left and had more records sent later, but the cupboard in the living room is still well stocked. There are about three hundred records. It was only a few years ago that Thomas Mann bought the record cabinet to keep his ever-growing collection in check. At that time, on the evening of January 27, 1948, his nephew had also been in the house and had moved the records into the compartments as soon as the cabinet was installed, whereupon Thomas Mann noted a "pleasing gain in order."

When news of the new tidiness in the old domicile reaches Thomas Mann in Switzerland, he is happy. And yet there is a hint of melancholy in his thoughts: "Can't believe yet that we don't want to return to the beautiful place," he notes in his diary.

In Pacific Palisades, the work continues. Since none of the children of the Mann family express an interest in the remaining collection of music, it is bequeathed to Klaus Pringsheim, and so the person who once brought in the records may now take them out again.

It's a very different story with the furniture. A portion is sent back to Switzerland. The rest is split between Thomas Mann's sons Golo and Michael, and what's left will be given to friends.

It doesn't take long, and the house on San Remo Drive is completely empty.

In other words, it's in an ideal condition for finally getting sold. The ads in the *Los Angeles Times* have certainly remained visible over the months, but now that Thomas Mann has left, the house has been cleared, and the estate agent is a woman, they are becoming a little—well, let's say more colorful.

A big "REDUCED!" will soon be part of the ads, even if no price is mentioned until mid-August. On August 17, 1952, however, things become more specific. "For a quickly decided buyer," it says in the paper, and then comes the price: "was $95,000—is now $72,500."

But because that still isn't enough, on August 31 the bar is raised once again. "Owner departed," it says now, followed on October 7 by a casual "Try for it!" Even this, however, does not bring the desired result, which is why the estate agent finds herself forced to reduce the price once again and offer the house for $62,000 on November 20 and—because nobody is biting—for $55,000 on November 23.

In Switzerland, the collapse of the price results in a fit of rage. "Miserable offers on the house in P. P.," Thomas Mann writes in his diary on December 14, while Michelle the real-estate agent tells the readers of the *Los Angeles Times* something completely different: "The Terrific Buy You Were Waiting For! Furniture Shipped to Europe. For Sale or Lease. 1550 San Remo Drive. The Chance of a Lifetime. No Fog. Full of Sunshine."

The nonexistent fog is a lie, of course, but so be it. This is America—
and getting the damn house sold is all that counts.

It isn't long before an interested party replies to the ad. They want to
pay $50,000—$35,000 upfront, in cash.

The offer is cabled to Europe and the answer is—yes.

"Relief from a burden and wounded feeling of final surrender never
to be seen again," Thomas Mann notes in his diary. And then, just
before Christmas, the words: "The beautiful house in California is
gone, sold off at half the price it's worth."

But just like that, Santa Claus brings a surprise that no one expected.
On December 28, the diary reports: "Strange that I forgot to note
the day before yesterday that the (bad) sale of the house over there
had been shattered by our tardiness."

In other words, Michelle the real-estate agent can continue to give
free rein to her creativity in composing newspaper ads. Whatever she
does, it's a new year after all—the perfect time to throw the old hon-
esty overboard and tackle it from the fantastic angle …

"1550 San Remo Drive. Fantastically Low Priced. Was $125,000, now
$55,000," proclaims the ad in the *Los Angeles Times* on January 2,
1953.

The house never cost that much, but who is to know? Anyone who
can save more than half of the original asking price will take it, even
if half the price is really the full price. Besides, whoever reads the ad
must start dreaming. Or swimming, since there is also said to be
"space for pool."

XXVI

Still, unfortunately, nobody replies—although this may be due to the fact that two days after New Year's Eve, most solvent customers are still so hungover that they aren't able to read the newspaper, which is why Michelle repeats the ad on January 14 and describes the house as "fantastically low priced." It'll be a piece of cake to find a buyer now!

In Switzerland, however, Thomas Mann doesn't feel like a piece of cake, since to the best of his knowledge business in America isn't exactly what he intended it to be, which is why on January 15 he writes in his diary: "The estate agent who produces frankly desperate and ineffective posters on the house won't get any replies from me."

But she doesn't need replies, at least not from Thomas Mann, because she is only waiting for one call—from whoever wants to buy the damn house.

On January 24, 1953, the agent makes a final attempt. "Best buys: 1550 San Remo. Riviera."

Then it's over.
There are no more ads.
Just waiting—and sorrow in Switzerland.

01. 26. 1953: "Homesick for the P. P. House."
03. 12. 1953: "In the evening talked with Katia about the question whether we did right, to leave California. One of my drawers filled with photographs that I can't look at in my current nervous state without my heart seizing up. I guess it's unreasonable. The house was all mine. I don't like this one."

07. 11. 1953: "Persistent homesickness for the P. P. House, one's own bathroom, the sofa in the study, etc. Often veritable fits of pain."

But that's not all. The pain is further aggravated by the fact that now, in July 1953, a buyer seems to have been found, but instead of the listed $55,000, they only want to pay $50,000, which leads in Switzerland to alternating fits of pain and rage.

But there's no point in resisting any further. These Americans will never change, and neither will he, Thomas Mann. So he takes what they offer him. On August 26, Thomas Mann signs the mandate of sale for the house on San Remo Drive at the American Consulate in Zurich. Two months later, he receives the corresponding check. The small sum annoys him, but the loss of the house hurts him infinitely more. His Californian chapter is thus finally closed, and in the great cash ledger of history, only a few melancholy memories and images remain—and slowly fade away. And yet: "It had to be like this, and it's fine now."

Acknowledgements

One wrote it, but many helped. Without the following people, this book would not have been possible. Without them, six thousand miles from 1550 San Remo Drive, I would not have been able to skip along the blank spaces that led me to Thomas Mann's house. That is why my heartfelt thanks go to you, the following.

Julie Dock, the granddaughter of Ted Löwenstein, who provided me with information about her grandfather and allowed me to print a small excerpt from our correspondence here.

Eva-Maria Herbertz, who provided invaluable help with my research on Paul Huldschinsky.

Susan Lamb of the Santa Monica Public Library, who searched the archives of local newspaper the *Palisadian* for articles about Thomas Mann; and Kathy Lo, librarian at the Santa Monica Public Library, who unearthed some photos for me.

Julia Larson, archivist at the University of California, Santa Barbara, who made the building plans of the house accessible, reviewed pictures, and provided information about J. R. Davidson.

Suzanne Oatey, archivist at the Huntington Library, who provided me with information on the estate of Eugene Swarzwald.

Dean Smith, archivist at the Bancroft Library, University of California, Berkeley, who showed me the way to Frederick Schiller Faust, aka Max Brand.

Randy Sakamoto, vice president of the board of directors of the Japanese Institute of Sawtelle, who sent me a photo of Koto and Wataru Shimidzu and connected me with some of their contemporaries.

Alan Nishio and his mother Mitsue Nishio, former detainees of the Manzanar War Relocation Center, who told me not only about Koto and Wataru Shimidzu, but also about life in the camp.

Paul Arbaugh, who gave me an impression of what life was like for Myrtle Chatman as a domestic worker.

Christian Herbart of the German Exile Archive, German National Library, who helped me find documents on Ernst Moritz Schlesinger.

Many thanks also to the Thomas Mann Archive, especially to Mr. Rolf Bolt; the E-Pics image database of the Swiss Federal Institute of Technology, Zurich; and the Monacensia Digital Library, Munich. The websites Ancestry, MyHeritage, and Fold3 were also a big help, and I found numerous historical documents in the database Newspapers.com. The Bremen passenger lists, which contain the data of many emigrants, were also very helpful in my research. I would also like to thank the forum participants of Baumkunde.de, who helped me to identify a series of flowers, shrubs, and trees growing on the property on San Remo Drive, based on historical photographs.

And last but not least, a thousand thanks to my daughter Anna, who used my computer to watch so many YouTube room tours that at some point I started taking these tours myself. Without her, I would never have had the idea to enter the house and its history in this way …

Chronology of the House

September 12, 1940   Thomas Mann buys a piece of land in the
                     so-called California Riviera District of
                     Pacific Palisades. The property is located on
                     San Remo Drive, is about sixty-five
                     thousand square feet, and costs $6,500.

January 4, 1941   First written mention of the architect Julius
                     Ralph Davidson in Thomas Mann's diary.
                     In the following months, Davidson drafts
                     plans for the house, which will be altered
                     numerous times.

April 9, 1941   The building application for the house at
                     1550 San Remo Drive is approved. Ernst
                     Schlesinger is named as general contractor in
                     the application, and E. Seiler as project
                     engineer. The planned size of the house is
                     144 × 43 feet.

June 21, 1941   Thomas and Katia Mann sign a contract
                     with Ernst Schlesinger for the construction
                     of the house.

July 2, 1941   The authorities grant permission for various
                     modifications to be made to the original
                     building plan. The size of the house is now
                     stated as 102 × 32 feet.

July 7, 1941   Groundbreaking ceremony for the house.

February 5, 1942	The Mann family moves into their new house on San Remo Drive.
June 24, 1952	Thomas and Katia Mann leave the house and move to Switzerland.
August 26, 1953	Sale of the house to the attorney Chester Lappen. Over the following years and decades, various conversions and extensions are carried out. A pool is constructed in the garden.
February 2012	After the death of Chester Lappen in December 2010, his family decides to rent out the house. In the following years, it is partly used as an Airbnb rental.
Summer 2016	The house is officially put up for sale.
November 2016	The Foreign Office of the Federal Republic of Germany acquires the house with the aim of creating a venue for transatlantic debate.
Spring 2017–Summer 2018	Renovation of the building and the property.
June 18, 2018	Opening of the Thomas Mann House. As part of the opening, a conference on "The Struggle for Democracy" is held at the Getty Center, Los Angeles, on June 19.

XXVII

SEBASTIAN STUMPF
SEVEN PALMS

The photographs in this book show the property at 1550 San Remo Drive, Pacific Palisades, Los Angeles. They were taken in January 2017, a few weeks after the property's purchase by the Federal Republic of Germany.

Francis Nenik lives with his family in Leipzig. He works as a Cross Golf guide, teaches civil engineers, and does a bit of farming. He also writes on the side. His recent publications include the essay "The Marvel of Biographical Bookkeeping" (translated by Katy Derbyshire, 2013), the novel *Coin-Operated History* (translated by Amanda DeMarco, 2017), and the narrative nonfiction book *Journey through a Tragicomic Century* (translated by Katy Derbyshire, 2020). From 2017 to 2021, he kept an online diary on the Trump presidency, which was published in German 2021.

Sebastian Stumpf is a visual artist. His photographs, video projections, and site-specific installations have been shown in various international exhibitions and he has received several awards, including a fellowship at the Villa Aurora in Los Angeles (2016). Most recently, during his stay at the Bauhaus in Dessau, he produced the video projection *Transitions #2 (Meisterhaus Schlemmer)*. He lives in Leipzig.

Imprint

Volume #1 of the series Volte Expanded, edited by Jörn Dege,
Mathias Zeiske, and Jan Wenzel

Concept: Francis Nenik, Sebastian Stumpf, Jan Wenzel
Photography: Sebastian Stumpf
Text: Francis Nenik
Translation: Jan Caspers
Editing: Jan-Frederik Bandel
Proofreading: Robert Dewhurst
Image editing: Jürgen Beck, ScanColor GmbH (cover image)
Graphic design: Ina Kwon
Printing: Gutenberg Beuys, Langenhagen

B/W illustrations: Julius Ralph Davidson Papers, Architecture
and Design Collection, Art, Design & Architecture Museum,
University of California, Santa Barbara

Published by
Spector Books
Harkortstraße 10
04107 Leipzig
www.spectorbooks.com

Distribution
Germany, Austria: GVA, Gemeinsame Verlagsauslieferung
Göttingen GmbH & Co. KG, www.gva-verlage.de
Switzerland: AVA Verlagsauslieferung AG, www.ava.ch
France, Belgium: Interart Paris, www.interart.fr

UK: Central Books Ltd, www.centralbooks.com
USA, Canada, Central and South America, Africa:
ARTBOOK | D.A.P., www.artbook.com
Japan: twelvebooks, www.twelve-books.com
South Korea: The Book Society, www.thebooksociety.org
Australia, New Zealand: Perimeter Distribution,
www.perimeterdistribution.com

Sebastian Stumpf thanks Katharina and Thierry Leduc,
Margit Kleinman, Friedel Schmoranzer, Dr. Claudia Gordon,
Annette Rupp, Dr. Markus Klimmer, Ursula Seeba-Hannan,
Dr. Andreas Görgen, Peter Schmitt, Julia Larson,
Timm Rautert, Thomas Fischer, Anna Vovan, Eduard Klein,
Jürgen Beck, and Jörg Obergfell.

This book was made possible by the generous support of
Katharina & Thierry Leduc.

It was further supported by the Villa Aurora; the Thomas
Mann House; Ursula Seeba-Hannan, LenzWerk; and Galerie
Thomas Fischer, Berlin.

First edition, 2021
Printed in Germany
ISBN 978-3-95905-335-8